ARDEN'S HOUSIN   ARY
5

Series Editors: Andrew Arden QC and Caroline Hunter

Alyson Kilpatrick is a practising barrister at Arden Chambers, specialising in housing, landlord and tenant, and local government law.

REPAIRS
AND MAINTENANCE

LAW AND PRACTICE
IN THE MANAGEMENT
OF SOCIAL HOUSING

Alyson Kilpatrick
BARRISTER

First published in Great Britain 1996 by

Lemos & Crane
20 Pond Square,
Highgate
London N6 6BA

Telephone 0181 348 8263

ISBN 1-898001-11-1

A CIP catalogue record for this book is
available from the British Library.

Designed by Mick Keates.
Typeset by Concise Artisans, London.
Printed by Redwood Books, Trowbridge.

ARDEN'S HOUSING LIBRARY

Series Editors: Andrew Arden QC and Caroline Hunter

"Ensuring the law is not just written but also
positively interpreted is important work.
I commend these titles."

Nick Raynsford MP, at the launch of Arden's Housing Library

"...an increasingly important series."
"The cumulative index is exceptionally good."

Housing (the journal of the Chartered Institute of Housing)

Volumes published in Arden's Housing Library

1 *Security of Tenure*
2 *Tenants' Rights*
3 *Nuisance and Harassment*
4 *Presenting Possession Proceedings*
5 *Repairs and Maintenance*
6 *Dealing with Disrepair*
7 CCT *of Housing Management (forthcoming)*

For more information about Arden's Housing Library,
please contact

Lemos & Crane
20 Pond Square
Highgate
London N6 6BA

Tel: 0181 348 8263
Fax: 0181 347 5740
Email: sales@lemos.demon.co.uk

CONTENTS

Table of Cases		xi
Table of Statutes		xv
FOREWORD by Andrew Arden QC		xvii

1	WHY REPAIR?	1
	Financial incentives	2
	Costs of litigation	2
	Legal requirements	4
	Social landlords	4
	Reasonableness	4

2	SOCIAL LANDLORD'S CONTRACTUAL LIABILITIES	7
	Is there a contract?	9
	Information	9
	Who is liable?	10
	Agents	10
	s11 Landlord and Tenant Act 1985	11
	Applicability	11
	Pre-24 October 1961	12
	Exclusions	12
	Structure and exterior	12
	Standard of repair	14
	Express contractual obligations	16
	Interpretation of express terms	16
	Implied contractual obligations	19
	Repair versus Renewal	19
	Conflict with express terms	22
	Common parts liability	22
	What is repair?	24
	Repair and improvement	25
	The test	25
	Alternative tests	30
	Redecoration	31
	Notice	31
	Notice to an agent	33
	"Reasonable time"	35
	Summary	35

3 SOCIAL LANDLORD'S NON-CONTRACTUAL   37
   LIABILITIES
   s4 Defective Premises Act 1972   39
   "Relevent defect"   40
   Notice   41
   "Premises"   43
   Occupiers Liability Act 1957   44
   s8 Landlord and Tenant Act 1985   45
   Applicability   45
   Breach of covenant for quiet enjoyment   46
   s1 Defective Premises Act 1972   47
   Nuisance   49
   Nuisance based on fault   50
   Remedies   50
   Negligence   50

4 COMMON TYPES OF COMPLAINTS   53
   Damp   53
   Penetrating damp   53
   Rising damp   55
   Condensation dampness   56
   Subsidence   57
   Roofs   58
   Asbestos   59
   Cockroaches and other insect infestation   60

5 TENANT'S REMEDIES   64
   Specific performance and injunctions   65
   Interim injunctions   66
   Limits to specific performance   67
   Resisting the application   68
   Evidence and agreeing the works   69
   Failure to carry out the works   70
   Damages   71
   Special damages   72
   General damages   73
   Interest   77
   Limitation periods   78
   Breach of contract   78
   Negligence   78
   Duty to mitigate   79
   Direct action   81

Set-off against rent 81
Set-off and counterclaims 82
Using rent to pay for repairs 84
Right to repair (secure tenants) 85
"Qualifying repairs" 86
Reporting repairs 86
"Prescribed periods" 87
Appointment of a receiver or manager 88

6 PUBLIC HEALTH DUTIES 90
Environmental Protection Act 1990 91
Statutory nuisance 91
Local authority duty to residents 93
Action by tenants 94
Procedure 99
Compensation orders 100
Appeals 102
Costs 102
Contingency fees 103
Other public health provisions 104
Sanitary facilities 104
Drains and sewers 105
Vermin 105
Fire precautions and dilapidation 105

7 TENANT'S CONTRACTUAL OBLIGATIONS 106
Tenant-like user 107
Acts of waste 108
Landlord's remedy 109
Landlord's remedies for breach 109
Possession of the premises 110
Damages 111
Injunctions 112

8 GETTING THE WORKS DONE 113
Right to enter to repair 114
Enforcement through injunction 115
Access to neighbouring land 115
Requiring tenant to move 116
Grounds for possession 117
Tenant's security of tenure 118
Payments to tenants 120

9 IMPROVEMENTS 123
  Improvements by tenant 123
    Statutory right to improve 124
    Compensation for improvements 125
    Rent following an improvement 126
  Improvements by landlord 126

10 COURT PROCEEDINGS 128
  Which court? 128
  Evidence 129
  Court etiquette 131
  Procedure 131
  Housing managers' evidence 132
  Experts' evidence 133
  Statutory nuisance in the magistrates' court 135
  Judgments and orders 135
  Conclusion 136

APPENDIX I: Checklist 137

APPENDIX II: Compendium of damages 141

APPENDIX III: Sample pleadings 155

APPENDIX IV: Glossary of terms 169

INDEX 175

TABLE OF CASES

Ali v Birmingham City Council June 1996 *Legal Action* 22   *152*
Andrews v Schooling (1991) 23 HLR 316   *48*

Barrett v Lounova (1982) Ltd [1989] 1 All ER 351   *20*
Berry & Avrisons Co Ltd March 1991 *Legal Action*   *147*
Birmingham DC v Kelly (1987) 19 HLR 452   *99*
Birmingham DC v McMahon (1987) 19 HLR 452   *95*
Bond v Chief Constable of Kent [1983] 1 All ER 456   *101*
Botross v London Borough of Hammersmith & Fulham (1994)
    24 HLR 299   *100*
British Anzani v International Marine [1979] 2 All ER 1073   *82*
British Waterways Board v Norman (1993) 26 HLR 232   *103*
Brown v Liverpool Corporation [1969] 3 All ER 1345   *14*

Calabar Properties v Stitcher [1984] 1 WLR 287   *72*
Camden Nominees v Forcey [1940] Ch 352   *72*
Clark v London Borough of Wandsworth June 1994 *Legal Action*   *63*
Clarke v Taff-Ely BC (1980) 10 HLR 44   *41*
Cook v Horford Investment Ltd and Mohammed Taj
    September 1992 *Legal Action*   *149*
Coventry City Council v Cartwright [1975] 1 WLR 845   *92*

Dadd v Christian Action (Enfield) Housing Association
    March 1994 *Legal Action*   *150*
Dinefwr Borough Council v Jones (1987) 19 HLR 445   *33*
Douglas-Scott v Scorgie [1984] 1 WLR 716   *13*
Dover DC v Farrar (1980) 2 HLR 32   *97*
Downie v London Borough of Lambeth July 1986
    Legal Action 95   *142*

Elmcroft Developments Ltd v Tankersley-Sawyer [1985]
    15 HLR 63   *27, 56*

Fairman v Perpetual Investment Building Society [1923] AC 74   45
Felix v Karachristos and Jachni August 1987 *Legal Action* 17   143

GLC v London Borough of Tower Hamlets (1983)
    15 HLR 54   98
Gordon v Selico (1986) 18 HLR 219   65
Greene v Chelsea Borough Council [1954] 2 QB 127   44
Griffin v Pillet [1926] 1 KB 17   33

Habinteg Housing Association v James (1994)
    27 HLR 299   21, 61-62
Hallett v London Borough of Camden August 1994
    Legal Action   150
Herbert v London Borough of Lambeth (1991) 24 HLR 299   101, 102
Hubble v London Borough of Lambeth April 1986
    Legal Action 50   142

Irvine v Moran (1990) 24 HLR 1   13, 30, 56

Johnson v Sheffield City Council (1994) *Current Law Week*
    18 February 1995   18
Jones v Derval Dampcoursing (1990) 8 CLR 128   146
Joyce v Liverpool City Council (1995) 27 HLR 548   3, 66

Kenning v Eve Construction [1989] 1 WLR 1189   134

Lasky v Webb March 1993 *Legal Action*   149
Lee-Parker v Izzet [1971] 1 WLR 1688   84
Lewin v London Borough of Brent March 1995
    Current Law Weekly   151
Liverpool County Council v Irwin [1977] AC 239   20, 23
Locabail International Finance Ltd v Agroexport [1986]
    1 All ER 901   67
London Borough of Brent v Carmel (1995) 27 HLR, CA   152
London Borough of Hackney v Carr (1994) *The Times* 9 March   100
London Borough of Haringey v Stewart (1991) 23 HLR 557   83
London Borough of Lambeth v Defreitas March 1994
    Legal Action   151
London Borough of Lambeth v Guerro March 1993
    Legal Action   149
London Borough of Lambeth v Williams December 1991
    Legal Action   148
London Borough of Newham v Hewitt June 1995 *Legal Action*   153
London Borough of Newham v Patel (1978) 13 HLR 77   15
Lubren v London Borough of Lambeth (1987) 20 HLR 166   74, 144

McCauley v Bristol City Council (1991) 23 HLR 586   *42*
McDougall v Easington District Council (1989)
    22 HLR 310   *28, 30, 121*
McGreal v Wake (1984) 13 HLR 107   *77, 116*
McLarty v London Borough of Islington October 1992
    Legal Action   *67*
McNerny v Lambeth LBC (1989) 21 HLR 188   *43*
Meah v London Borough of Tower Hamlets October 1986
Legal Action 135   *143*
Miller v Emcer Products Ltd [1956] Ch 304   *22*
Minchburn v Peck (1987) 20 HLR 392   *31, 80, 144*
Mira v Ayler Square Investments Ltd (1990) 22 HLR 182   *47*
Morris v Liverpool City Council (1987) 20 HLR 498, CA   *35*

National Coal Board v Neath BC [1976] 1 WLR 543   *93*
New England Properties Ltd v Portsmouth Shops Ltd [1993]
    1 EGLR 84   *59*

O'Brien v Robinson [1973] AC 912   *31*

Palmer v Sandwell Metropolitan Borough Council (1985)
    20 HLR 74   *17*
Parish v Leslie August 1994 *Legal Action*   *150*
Parker v London Borough of Camden [1986] Ch 162   *67*
Parker v London Borough of Camden [1985] 2 All ER 141   *88*
Personal Representatives of Chiodi v de Marney (1988)
    21 HLR 6   *74-75, 146*
Proudfoot v Hart (1890) 25 QBD 42   *24*

Quick v Taff-Ely Borough Council [1986] QB 809   *29*

R v Chappell [1984] Crim LR 574   *101*
R v Cooper [1982] Crim LR 308   *101*
R v Thomson Holidays [1973] QB 592   *102*
R v Vivian [1979] 1 All ER 48   *101*
R v Wandsworth County Court, ex p. Munn (1994) 26 HLR 697   *70*
Ravenseft Properties Ltd v Davstone (Holdings) Ltd [1980]
    QB 12   *26*
Rees v Davies September 1987 *Legal Action*   *144*
Rimmer v Liverpool City Council [1985] QB 1   *52*
Robbins v Jones (1863) 15 CB (NS) 221   *22*

Sharpe v Manchester City Council (1977) 5 HLR 73, CA   *62*
Sheldon v West Bromwich Corporation (1973) 13 HLR 23, CA   *35*

Shirlaw v Southern Foundries (1926) Ltd [1939] 2 KB 206   *19*
Smith v Bradford Metropolitan Council (1982) 4 HLR 86   *43*
Staves v Leeds City Council (1990) 23 HLR 10730, 56
Stratton and Porter v Arakpo and London Borough of Southwark
    June 1991 *Legal Action*   *148*
Sturolson & Co v Mauroux (1988) 20 HLR 332   *74, 145*
Sullivan v Johnson March 1992 *Legal Action* 13   *148*

Taylor v Knowsley Borough Council (1985) 17 HLR 376, CA   *142*
Televantos v McCulloch (1990) 23 HLR 412   *83, 147*
The Trustees of the Dame Margaret Hungerford Charity v Beazley
    (1994) 26 HLR 269   *54*
Thompson v Birmingham City Council September 1990
    Legal Action   *147*
Thompson v Elmbridge DC [1987] 1 WLR 1425   *9*
Trustees of Calthorpe Edgbaston Estate v Routledge December 1991
    Legal Action   *148*

Wainwright v Leeds City Council (1984) 13 HLR 117   *16*
Warner v London Borough of Lambeth (1984) 15 HLR 42   *96*
Warren v Keene [1954] 1 QB 15   *107*
Wringe v Cohen [1940] 1 KB 229   *50*

Yilmaz v London Borough of Hackney March 1995 *Legal Action*   *76*
Yorston & Yorston v Crewfield Ltd and Others July 1985
    Legal Action   *88, 142*

Zone Properties v Painter June 1987 *Legal Action* 21   *143*

TABLE OF STATUTES

Access to Neighbouring Land
Act 1992   *115*

Building Act 1984
  s 21   *105*
  s 59   *105*
  s 64   *104*

County Courts Act 1984
  s 38   *67*
  s 69   *77*

Defective Premises Act 1972
  s 1   *38, 47-48, 79*
  s 3   *48*
  s 4   *38, 39-44*
  s 4(1)   *39*
  s 4(2)   *40*

Environmental Protection Act
1990
  Part III   *91-104*
  s 79   *91, 93*
  s 79(1)(a)   *91*
  s 79(1)(g)   *99*
  s 79(7)   *92, 95*
  s 80   *91*
  s 81   *91*
  s 82   *99, 102*
  s 82(1)   *94*
  s 82(3)   *99*
  s 82(4)   *94*
  s 82(5)   *99*

s 82(8)   *100*
s 82(12)   *103*
Schedule 3   *93*

Housing Act 1985
  s 96   *75*
  s 97   *124*
  s 99   *124*
  s 100   *126*
  s 101   *126*
  s 104   *10*
  Schedule 2   *110*

Housing Act 1988
  s 35(4)(d)   *119*
  Schedule 2   *111*

Land Compensation Act 1973
121

Landlord and Tenant Act 1985
  s 8   *38, 45-46*
  s 11   *3, 7-9, 11-16, 19-22, 31*
  s 11(1A)   *22, 27*
  s 11(1)(a)   *11, 12*
  s 11(1)(b)   *11*
  s 11(1)(c)   *11*
  s 11 (2)   *12*
  s 11(6)   *114*
  s 17   *65-66*

Landlord and Tenant Act 1987
89

Leasehold Reform, Housing
and Urban Development Act
1993
  s 121   *85*
  s 122   *125*

Limitation Act 1980   *78*

Local Government and
Housing Act 1989   *3*

Magistrates' Courts Act 1980
  101
  s 35   *102*

Occupiers Liability Act 1957
  38, 44-45

Powers of Criminal Courts Act
1973
  s 35   *100*

Public Health Act 1936
  s 83   *105*

Supreme Court Act 1981
  s 37   *88-89*

FOREWORD

by Andrew Arden QC

Alyson Kilpatrick's *Repairs and Maintenance* is, in one sense, but one more in the Housing Library through which we seek to evolve the notion that – in a climate of reduced public expenditure available *both* for housing itself *and* for tenants or other occupiers to enjoy access to qualified advice and assistance to enforce their rights – it is important for housing managers to ensure that their actions are legally correct from the outset instead of relying on a corrective response from occupiers: see "Social Housing: Moving from Litigation to Managerial Prevention of Errors," *Leading Edge* (Lemos & Crane Occasional Briefing No. 1; also reproduced as the Series Foreword in S. Belgrave, *Nuisance and Harassment*, Vol. 3 in the Library).

In the case of disrepair, this message is, perhaps, more important than in any other. If the property of social landlords falls into disrepair, then a court will order works on an individual unit basis, and may well award substantial sums of damages to the individual tenant (and costs of legal representation which may likewise prove substantial). There has, indeed been some media attention paid to the phenomenon, in consequence of which some local authorities have found that significant proportions of their maintenance budgets have gone, not – as intended – to planned or preventative maintenance, but to reactive repairs, compensation and costs, with the consequence that large-scale, estatewide programmes have not been able to proceed. For cyclical repairs, read cycle of frustration and decay.

In times of severely constrained expenditure, one is bound to feel considerable sympathy for social landlords who bemoan this Catch-22: if they await the programme, the individual complainant can use the law to achieve a priority that in turn delays improved conditions for others; yet, there is not the money to bring forward the programme. There is, of course, no grand solution – other than for the government to provide more money or else to lower legal standards (as, e.g., most mandatory grants in respect of unfit property are due to be repealed when the Housing Grants, etc., Bill becomes law). The first appears to be out of the question; to resort to the second would be some kind of ultimate defeat for those who have committed themselves to the provision of decent, social housing; to allow our difficulties to persuade us to support any such regression would be to turn upon our own.

Yet just because there is no grand solution does not mean that there is nothing that can be done to mitigate a difficult problem. There is. If housing managers are actively aware of what legal rights tenants and other occupiers enjoy, below which their standards cannot fall without the risk of costly litigation and even costlier reactive repairs, they can better allocate their resources – financial and human – to ensure that there is a sustainable balance between those rights and the needs of the programme. At one extreme, throwing all one's resources into the programme could render it vulnerable to upset as a result of a single substantial claim (of which legal costs alone may be a significant proportion); at the other, throwing all one's resources into individual claims is a form of crisis management that can only, in the longer term, postpone and exacerbate the problem.

To illustrate: one (large) social landlord established a Task Force, to ring-fence and react *immediately* to complaints of disrepair which appeared to be capable of pursuit to law (whether by way of civil action in the county court, or criminal action for statutory nuisance in the magistrates' court): within days, property would be visited, those works to which it was considered there was a legal entitlement to an immediate order were commissioned, and within – at the outside – weeks, they were executed. Contemporaneously, an offer of compensation was made, representing a fair – but not excessive – sum for the period in question. Likewise, legal costs (if any) *to date* were offered. Actions that traditionally had led to consequences – globally – in the five figures could be contained in the low fours. Meanwhile, the longer-term works could be absorbed in the next appropriate programme.

What was imaginative about this solution was the admixture of legal and building professional skills. A lawyer worked in the Task Force, to advise on what works would be the subject of an immediate order, and what would represent fair compensation and an appropriate payment for costs; surveyors advised the lawyer on the condition of the property, the consequences and implications, and organised the maintenance crews; it was a team response to a multi-disciplinary activity that *could* not await the normal "channels of communication and co-operation" that prevailed in a big organisation, without generating a financial consequence that took the landlord straight (back) into that cycle of frustration and decay to which I referred above.

All of which is a rather lengthy explanation of why it is only in one sense that this is but one more in the series; for alongside this book is published Patrick Reddin's *Dealing with Disrepair*. Mr Reddin is a surveyor – there need be no secret of the matter, he is a very *good* surveyor, and he has for many years been my very good friend! For many years, he has also been the leading surveyor who has given expert evidence for tenants around the capital as to the repairs to which they are entitled. He has enjoyed a remarkable, perhaps unparalleled, court-room success. And he has been highly active in the repair and improvement (and construction) of social housing. In his book, he has sought to bring together his areas of long experience, so as to enable housing managers to do their jobs in a way that accords with their tenants' legal rights, and ensure that those rights do not cut across the way that they wish to do their jobs.

This book and Mr Reddin's accordingly mirror the theme of this series (and this Foreword) by explaining to housing managers how to identify disrepair, and to commission its remedy, in the context of the legal framework by which the subject is governed. Between them, these books and their authors have taken forward the notion that "prevention is better than cure", in two disciplines, entirely different conceptually, but entirely dependent on each other for their daily application. This one is the theory; Mr Reddin's book, the practice.

Andrew Arden QC
Arden Chambers
59 Fleet Street
London EC4Y 1JU

CHAPTER 1

WHY REPAIR?

Financial incentives / *Costs of litigation* / **Legal requirements** / *Social landlords* / *Reasonableness*

The physical condition of the properties in which people live has always been a matter of great social concern and importance. Many of the council houses built both before and after the second world war were intended to improve on the appalling conditions of the private sector stock in which millions were then living. How ironic then if those very homes intended to replace the slums of their day, become the slums of today. Yet it is certainly the case that social rented housing stock does suffer from some severe problems of disrepair. The 1991 *English House Condition Survey* (HMSO 1993) estimated that to remedy defects in the English social rented housing stock would cost £780m of public resources.

Readers are also referred to P. Reddin *Dealing with Disrepair* Arden's Housing Library, vol. 6, 1996, which provides guidance for social landlords on the practical inspection and diagnosis of disrepair problems.

Financial incentives

Good housing management always looks to the welfare of tenants as one of the main priorities. Maintaining the health, safety and comfort of tenants provides an answer in itself as to why repairs should be carried out promptly and effectively. Furthermore it makes much sense in financial terms for social landlords to repair. While many local authorities, and increasingly, housing associations have seen their budgets tightened, there may be a false economy in failing to carry out routine maintenance and early repair. If such work is not carried out in good time the eventual cost of the repairs will be much greater, eating further into limited budgets.

If the property of social landlords does fall into disrepair, a court may well order repairs on an individual unit basis. This can disrupt the longer term proposals to phase in a large scale, estate wide, programme of maintenance and repair. This places a greater short term burden onto the landlord with associated escalated costs.

A well repaired and maintained stock will undoubtedly lead to better relations between the landlord and tenants, leading to fewer demands from tenants and less drain on staff time. Badly maintained estates can lead to a deteriorating environment for tenants, with consequent higher rates of voids and rent arrears.

Costs of litigation
The context of this book, however, is the legal liability which underpins the requirement to repair. Failure to comply with this legal liability can also lead to an extra financial burden. The cases in Appendix II indicate the

large sums of compensatory damages which may be awarded for periods during which the premises remain in a state of disrepair. Dealing with complaints and any subsequent litigation is a drain on staff and resources; it is better to have efficient mechanisms to respond promptly to the complaint. Since the advent of the Local Government and Housing Act 1989, local authorities are charged with balancing their Housing Revenue Account, and added expenditure on litigation may result in increased rents across the stock or cut backs in other areas. Similarly tight funding for housing associations means that management cannot permit the drain on resources caused by protracted disputes with tenants over repairs.

The judgment in *Joyce v Liverpool City Council* (1995) 27 HLR 548, warns about the waste of time and money on litigation rather than the repairs themselves: "The evidence before us does suggest that court trial of minor section 11 [Landlord and Tenant Act 1985] claims yields a benefit to the legal profession out of all proportion to that gained by the tenant and diverts the funds of local authority landlords from purposes more germane to their public function."

Appendix III sets out in detail a typical example of a landlord's defence to a tenant claiming damages for breach of repairing obligation. (In addition, a summary and checklist of procedures for landlords is provided in Appendix I. A glossary of terms is provided in Appendix IV.)

Legal requirements

As this book sets out to illustrate, social landlords are under a considerable legal requirement to repair their stock. The existing law governing the repairing obligations of landlords and tenants is a complex mix of contract, statute and tort. The aim of this book is to examine the extent of the current obligations – largely covenants or statutory duties to repair – and to give guidance on the conduct of proposed and actual complaints, both before and after the issue of court proceedings. In addition this book considers the law governing the enforcement of the obligations. The problems arising with social housing stock and the solutions required are essentially practical. There are several legal avenues which a tenant may use against social housing landlords to remedy disrepair to his or her home and this book will seek to place these various legal actions in their appropriate context and give guidance on the practical and legal responses to be made by social housing landlords.

Social landlords

In general no distinction needs to be drawn between whether the social landlord is a local authority (or other public authority such as a housing action trust, or development corporation) or a housing association. The common law remedies in contract and tort are not concerned with the particular status of the landlord. The book does not include those legal remedies which are primarily concerned with local authority enforcement against the private sector, i.e. the legislation relating to unfitness, service of repair notices on private sector landlords/owner occupiers and closing orders. All of these subjects are dealt with in A. Dymond *Houses in Multiple Occupation* Arden's Housing Library (forthcoming). However, in chapter 6 there is a discussion about repairs and maintenance which arise under the public health legislation. Tenants in particular may seek to take action under the provisions relating to statutory nuisance in order to deal with the disrepair problems.

The book also sets out the obligations on the tenant to repair and maintain the property, and the many problems which can arise – of access, compensation and security of tenure – when the social landlord does set out to carry out works.

Reasonableness

While this book is concerned primarily with the application of the law to disrepair, this is not, and can never be, a scientific exercise. Those dealing with social housing and the maintenance of the stock may be forgiven for thinking that the law has little to do with the merits of a given situation. This is not the case. So many of the legal remedies available to tenants are within the judge's discretion. In the exercise of that discretion he or she will be concerned with the reasonableness of both parties' conduct. If it can be shown that the landlord has acted reasonably and done all that can reasonably be expected in the circumstances, the judge is more likely to want to find in the landlord's favour.

Judges live in the real world and appreciate more than many might suppose just what constraints a social landlord may be acting within.

At all times the landlord must *act* reasonably and be

seen to act reasonably. If this is the case it is unlikely that landlords and housing managers will be the subject of judicial criticism and disfavour to the extent that is currently experienced in the local courts.

CHAPTER 2

SOCIAL LANDLORD'S CONTRACTUAL LIABILITIES

Is there a contract? / **Information** / **Who is liable?** / *Agents* / **s11 Landlord and Tenant Act 1985** / *Applicability* / *Pre-24 October 1961* / *Exclusions* / *Structure and exterior* / *Standard of repair* / **Express contractual obligations** / *Interpretation of express terms* / **Implied contractual obligations** / *Repair versus renewal* / *Conflict with express terms* / **Common parts liability** / **What is repair?** / *Repair and improvement* / *The Test* / *Alternative tests* / *Redecoration* / **Notice** / *Notice to an Agent* / *"Reasonable time"* / **Summary**

There are two kinds of repairing obligation: those set out in the contract itself and those imported into it by law.

Everyone working in the field of social housing has heard of section 11 of the Landlord and Tenant Act 1985. This imposes repairing obligations on a landlord whether they are set out in the tenancy agreement or not (section 11 is dealt with in detail in this chapter) and it is easy to assume that this statutory provision governs the whole of the landlord's obligations. This is not correct. It is dangerous to attach any lesser importance to the written terms of the tenancy agreement.

The tenancy agreement should always be the starting point for consideration where there is a dispute as to the extent of a tenant's entitlement to repairs. While section 11 implies obligations into the tenancy agreement as terms of the contract, any *express* terms which are more extensive will still take priority.

There is little a social landlord can do with respect to terms imposed by Parliament, however, a landlord *can* exercise control over the express terms.

If a landlord does not wish to extend a tenant's entitlement then care is required to ensure that the tenancy agreement does not inadvertently give more than the law requires. If the lawyers or policy makers do wish to extend tenant's rights, housing managers – those charged with the daily implementation of agreements – must understand the nature and scope of the increased rights.

This chapter considers those terms which are incorporated into every tenancy agreement regardless of what is intended; those which remain within the landlord's control; and, terms which may or may not be incorporated depending on the particular circumstances.

The terms implied by section 11 of the Landlord and Tenant Act 1985 are discussed first of all because they provide a minimum requirement in the case of most contracts. More extensive express terms are then considered. Finally, common law implied terms are examined for those situations where section 11 may not apply. Guidance is given on the particular liability for disrepair of common parts in blocks of flats. Having established the extent of contractual obligations to repair, this chapter then sets out what is meant by a liability to repair and the extent of that requirement. In most circumstances social landlords will not be under any liability to repair unless the disrepair has been brought to its attention. The final section of the chapter examines the requirement of notice.

Only by fully understanding the legal rights which tenants enjoy and the minimum standard of repair and maintenance required by the law can social landlords hope to achieve a balance between their planned pro-grammes of works and compliance with obligations on an individual basis. Some complaints will require im-mediate attention and remedy; others can be dealt with by inclusion in a large scale programme.

Is there a contract?

In order for repairing obligations to arise in contract there must, of course, be an existing tenancy agreement between the social landlord and the tenant. In most cases this will not be problematic. One situation where this might be in doubt is where a suspended possession order has been obtained against the tenant and there has been a breach of the terms of the order. It can be argued that there is no tenancy following the breach of a suspended order (*Thompson v Elmbridge DC* [1987] 1 WLR 1425).

Information

Secure tenants must be provided with information about the extent of the landlord's repairing obligations, whether express or implied (section 104 of the Housing Act 1985). Housing associations should also give such information to their assured tenants under the terms of the Tenants' Guarantee. See further C. Hunter, *Tenants' Rights*, ch. 5, Arden's Housing Library, vol. 2, 1995.

Who is liable?

It makes no difference whether the social landlord has contracted out management of the repairs or maintenance to a third party – a situation that may become increasingly common with compulsory competitive tendering. Where there is a contractual liability to repair, it is no defence to argue that "arrangements were made for an agent to ensure repairs were carried out." The social landlord will still be responsible to the tenant, who will be entitled to damages for any losses caused by a failure to comply with the tenancy agreement. The tenant is not concerned with how the social landlord has arranged to fulfil the terms and does not need to add the agents to any claim.

Agents
Where an agent has become responsible for ensuring that repairs are carried out the landlord may seek to recover any damages that have to be paid to a tenant. This would be done by an action against the agent for failure to comply with the agency agreement. Whether the blame can be laid at the door of the agent will depend on the terms of the agreement and the facts of any particular case. Action against an agent can be taken in a separate action; or alternatively it may be

simpler in some cases where the evidence will overlap for the landlord to seek to add the agent to the tenant's action as a third party.

s11 Landlord and Tenant Act 1985

Section 11 of the Landlord and Tenant Act 1985 (as amended) implies a clause into leases of dwelling-houses granted for less than seven years on or after 24 October 1961 that the landlord will :

1. keep the structure and exterior (which includes drains, gutters and external pipes) of the dwelling-house in repair – section 11(1)(a);

2. keep the installations for the supply of water, gas, electricity and sanitation in the dwelling-house in repair and proper working order – section 11(1)(b); and

3. keep the installations in the dwelling-house for space heating and heating water in repair and proper working order – section 11(1)(c).

Applicability

As section 11 applies to all tenancies for less than seven years, this includes all periodic tenancies, weekly, monthly or quarterly, even though they may last for more than seven years. Where the dwelling-house is a flat and the tenancy agreement was entered into on or after 15 January 1989, section 11 (as amended) also requires that the landlord keeps the structure and ex-terior of the building in which the flat is situated, and its installations, in repair as long as: (a) the landlord owns or has control of the part of the building con-cerned; and (b) the disrepair affects the tenant's enjoyment of his or her dwelling house or the common parts of the building (see further pp. 22-23 and 46-47 below).

Pre-24 October 1961
For leases which started prior to 24 October 1961 the repairing obligation will depend on what was actually agreed between the parties. A similar term may be implied in the absence of any agreement (see below, pp. 19-22).

Exclusions
The implied statutory covenant does not require the landlord:
1. to carry out works for which the tenant would be liable under the latter's duty to use the premises in a tenant-like manner, or would be so liable but for an express covenant on his or her part;
2. to rebuild or reinstate premises destroyed or damaged by fire, tempest, flood or other inevitable accident; or
3. to keep in repair or maintain anything which the lessee is entitled to remove from the dwelling-house: section 11(2) of the Landlord and Tenant Act 1985.

Structure and exterior
The obligation under section 11(1)(a) is to keep the structure and exterior in repair. Structure and exterior do not have a precise legal meaning. The words will cover anything which in the ordinary course of things would be considered as part of the structure or exterior of a dwelling house. Thus, something may be part of the structure and exterior even where it does not form part of the dwelling formally leased to the tenant. See

further P. Reddin *Dealing with Disrepair*, p. 2, Arden's Housing Library vol. 6, 1996.

Case report
The tenant occupied the top (third floor) flat in a building and the roof above the flat was in disrepair. The question the court had to decide was whether the roof was part of the structure and exterior of "the dwelling-house". The Court of Appeal said that the question had to be decided by reference to the ordinary meaning of the words, asking whether the roof would be regarded as an integral part of the flat, even if was not part of the letting to the tenant. The court drew a distinction between flat roofs which were an integral part of the structure and a case in which there is a void space or an uninhabited loft between the top floor flat and roof, which may be borderline. *Douglas-Scott v Scorgie* [1984] 1 WLR 716

"Structure"

The term "structure" has been interpreted by the courts to mean "the elements of the overall dwelling-house which give it its essential appearance, stability and shape...a particular element must be a material or significant element in the overall construction." (*Irvine v Moran* (1990) 24 HLR 1). Structure includes walls (outside walls and inner party walls), roofs, windows (including frames), ceilings and so on. It does not include internal wall plaster or decorations – but these will often be affected by other disrepair, for example where damaged by penetrating damp.

"Exterior"

Exterior means the outside or external parts of a dwelling – but will not include outside paving. However, external steps and a path leading up to a house may be included if they are the only means of access to the house (*Brown v Liverpool Corporation* [1969] 3 All ER 1345). Each case will be looked at on its own facts. The court will decide whether in all the circumstances the item, sought to be included by the tenant as part of the exterior or structure, forms an essential part of the building.

Disrepair must be to the structure or exterior. This means:

• damage which is not structural will not be covered by section 11, for example black mould (*Irvine v Moran* (1992) 24 HLR 1)

• defects in the building resulting from bad design will not be covered if they do not cause a physical defect in the structure and exterior. For example the Court of Appeal decided that condensation dampness caused by a design defect in a building did not fall within section 11, since there was no actual disrepair to any element of the structure or exterior of the building (*Quick v Taff-Ely Borough Council* [1986] QB 809 – see further pp. 29 and 30, below, on condensation dampness).

Standard of repair

The standard of repair required by section 11 of the Landlord and Tenant Act 1985 will be determined having regard to the age, character and prospective life of the dwelling and also of the locality in which it is situated. In other words the standard to which the property is to be repaired will primarily be judged by its age and condition at the date of the letting. While this can be said to be the rule it is not always rigidly applied. (See further P. Reddin *Dealing with Disrepair*, ch. 7, p. 119 and pp. 124-128, Arden's Housing Library vol. 6, 1996.) Changes in the character of a neighbourhood during the letting may result in this test being held to be inappropriate.

Case report

In 1973 Mr Patel moved into a house owned by the London Borough of Newham. The house was in a very poor condition, as it was scheduled for redevelopment. The rent was low to reflect the poor condition. Mr Patel applied to be transferred, but no other accommodation was available. In 1977 an environmental health officer reported that the house was unfit for habitation. In the light of the report the council considered that the house should no longer be occupied, as temporary repairs were not a viable option. Alternative accommodation was offered to Mr Patel but it was turned down. The council then sought possession of Mr Patel's home. Mr Patel counterclaimed for breach of the repairing covenant under what is now section 11 of the Landlord and Tenant Act 1985.

The Court of Appeal found that, having regard to the prospective life of the property, there was no breach of the repairing covenant. The council was not liable to carry out repairs which would prove wholly fruitless. *London Borough of Newham v Patel* (1978) 13 HLR 77

It has been suggested that social landlords should maintain a higher standard of repair than private landlords. The court has rejected this argument: the standard of repairs imposed on public sector landlords is no different to that imposed on private sector landlords (*Wainwright v Leeds City Council* (1984) 13 HLR 117).

Express contractual obligations

With the exceptions of certain implied terms such as the landlord's repairing covenant contained in section 11 of the Landlord and Tenant Act 1985 (see above, p. 11) and the lessee's covenant of tenant-like user (i.e. to act as a reasonable tenant, see p. 107, below) which are implied into all tenancies covered by this book, the parties remain free to include express clauses of their own choosing.

While section 11 cannot be excluded by a public sector landlord by an express clause, some terms recorded in tenancy agreements extend beyond the boundaries of section 11 and their meaning may be disputed.

Interpretation of express terms

The interpretation of an express obligation is a question of fact in each case and depends on the individual wording. To be able to rely on such an obligation it must first be established that the term was properly incorporated into the agreement. So, for example, where an express repairing clause has apparently been added to the tenancy agreement after the commencement of the tenancy, the proper procedures for making changes must have been followed. (See further

C. Hunter *Tenants' Rights*, ch. 4, Arden's Housing Library vol. 2, 1995 for a discussion of how social landlords may alter the terms of their agreements.)

Case report
A tenant of Sandwell Borough Council relied on a variation to her lease which sought to make the local authority liable for design defects (not included within section 11). However the statutory procedure for variation of such leases was not properly followed and the Court of Appeal therefore held that the term was not incorporated into the agreement and the tenant could not derive any benefit from it. *Palmer v Sandwell Metropolitan Borough Council* (1988) 20 HLR 74

A tenant may also seek to enforce a promise made or a warranty given by the landlord which is not contained in the tenancy agreement. This may occur if the landlord has given an assurance prior to the signing of the agreement and the signing was made conditional upon it. For example, where a landlord promises to repair defective guttering as a precondition of the tenant entering into occupation and then fails to carry out the repair, the tenant could take legal action to enforce the promise.

It is important that both parties are aware of the repairing obligations in the lease. In some instances public sector landlords will include in a tenancy agreement an express term which is in fact more generous than those implied by statute. Great care must be taken that housing managers or officers dealing with complaints or lawyers involved in litigation or threatened litigation examine the express terms which have been agreed.

Case report
The tenancy agreement used by Sheffield City Council not only included the repairing obligations under the Landlord and Tenant Act 1985 but also a covenant that the council would provide a house that was "fit to live in." The house in question suffered severe condensation dampness and mould growth. The court decided that this term imported the minimum fitness standard for human habitation as contained in section 604 of the Housing Act 1985 and went on to use that as a checklist. The house did not measure up to this standard and the tenant was awarded damages. Given that damages for condensation problems and mould are not generally covered by the section 11 repairing obligation (see below p. 24 on the meaning of repair) the express clause clearly gave the tenant much greater rights than would normally be the case. *Johnson v Sheffield City Council* (1994) *Current Law Week* 18 February 1995

Finally, whatever the wording of an express repairing obligation, it will never be construed to require a landlord to renew the entire property. The landlord will never be compelled to turn an old and decaying property into a new or completely sound property. The repairing obligation will be interpreted having regard to the condition that the property was in at the commencement of the tenancy.

Implied contractual obligations

Repair versus Renewal

The repairing obligations of social landlords will generally be established by the express terms of the agreement and by the terms implied by section 11 of the Landlord and Tenant Act 1985. In certain circumstances it may be relevant to consider, however, whether any further terms may be implied into the tenancy agreement by common law. It will be particularly important where the tenancy was granted prior to 1961 because terms implied by section 11 do not apply. This will be the case with situations which fall outside the ambit of section 11.

A lease gives rise to what is essentially a contractual relationship. It is therefore subject to the general principles governing terms that may be implied as part of a contract. A term may be implied as a matter of fact or of law. If implied as a *matter of fact* it will only be because it is "so obvious that it goes without saying..." (*Shirlaw v Southern Foundries (1926) Ltd* [1939] 2 KB 206). One way of describing the test would be whether the parties themselves, on discovering the absence of the proposed term, would react with surprise that the term was not within the agreement which they all believed had already recorded their actual intentions.

When a term is implied as a *matter of law* it will take effect irrespective of the intentions of the parties because it is considered that such a term ought to be implied either into every contract of its kind as a matter of policy or to the particular contract which is in dispute before the court.

For a term to be implied it must be necessary for the

proper performance of the contract and one which would have been agreed to by the parties (assuming them to be reasonable people) if it had been pointed out to them at the time. It is not sufficient to say that the term would make the contract a better or fairer one.

These general contractual principles have been applied to tenancy agreements in order to imply a term that the landlord should maintain in reasonable repair the common parts of a high rise block of flats in circumstances where the landlord retained control of the common parts and their lighting – see further below pp. 22 to 24 on common parts (*Liverpool County Council v Irwin* [1977] AC 239).

Case report

The tenant had succeeded to a tenancy agreement entered into by her father in 1941. The lease contained an express term that the tenant would carry out all internal repairs to the premises but was silent about any obligation in respect of external repairs. The Court of Appeal accepted the tenant's argument that in order to make sense of the agreement an obligation to carry out repairs to the exterior of the premises must be placed on someone. As the tenant had only expressly contracted to undertake repairs to the interior it would be wrong, as a matter of construction, to impose the added obligation to repair the exterior on the tenant. It was held to be inappropriate to place such a burden on a monthly tenant. Kerr LJ held that "the only solution which makes business sense" is an implied obligation on the landlord to carry out external repairs. *Barrett v Lounova (1982) Ltd* [1989] 1 All ER 351

Case report

Habinteg Housing Association owned an estate made up of 91 dwellings situated along five roads. Mrs James was the tenant in a block on the estate which comprised three flats. Each flat was self contained and had its own separate access. The tenant had moved into her flat in February 1986. Soon after the move, she discovered the flat was infested by cockroaches. Other tenants on the estate also suffered infestation. No effective action was taken until the local authority served an abatement notice on the housing association under section 83 of the Public Health Act 1936. As a result it was decided to treat the entire area of infestation, as opposed to the piece-meal process previously tried. The treatment was successful and from September 1991 onwards the tenant suffered no further infestation.

The housing association took proceedings against the tenant for arrears of rent. She counterclaimed for damages on several bases including breach of an implied term that it was the duty of the landlord to "take reasonable care to abate an infestation arising on the estate which could not be abated other than by the landlord taking timeous action in respect of all or any of a group of dwellings on the estate."

The judge dismissed the tenant's counterclaim and she appealed. The Court of Appeal would not imply the term suggested by the tenant for three reasons. The term lacked clarity of expression; it was not so obvious as to go without saying; and thirdly, the contract would still be fully effective without it. *Habinteg Housing Association v James* (1994) 27 HLR 299

Certain obligations, such as the implied covenant that the landlord guarantees the tenant quiet enjoyment of the land, are read into all tenancy agreements. However, there is no obligation universally implied into tenancy agreements that the landlord keeps the property in repair. Unless it can be shown to be required to give "business efficacy" to the contract (as in *Barrett v Lounova*, see p. 20 above) the court will not automatically imply such a term into the contract. In the much cited case of *Robbins v Jones* (1863) 15 CB (NS) 221, Erle CJ stated the basic principle: "There is no law against letting a tumble-down house; and the tenant's remedy is upon his contract, if any." In general the courts are therefore reluctant to imply obligations into tenancy agreements which go beyond that of section 11 of the Landlord and Tenant Act 1985.

Conflict with express terms

It is a generally accepted principle of contract law that an express term, even a limited term, will operate so as to prevent the inclusion of a more comprehensive implied term (*Miller v Emcer Products Ltd.* [1956] Ch 304).

Common parts liability

Prior to the Housing Act 1988, the covenant contained in section 11 of the Landlord and Tenant Act 1985 did not refer to the common parts of a building in which a dwelling may be situated.

Section 11(1A) of the Landlord and Tenant Act 1985 (as amended by the Housing Act 1988) now imposes liability on landlords for the maintenance and repair of the common parts of buildings where the dwelling forms part only of a larger building. This is increasingly relied on by tenants living in blocks of flats. The amendments will not apply, however, to leases granted before 15 January 1989 or contracts made before that date. Accordingly, in relation to common parts under tenancies pre-dating 15 January 1989, there is no statutorily implied covenant to keep them in repair.

Tenants may, however, still seek to rely on the decision in *Liverpool City Council v Irwin* [1977] AC 239 (noted above) where in order to give the tenancy business efficacy a covenant to maintain in reasonable repair had to be implied. This covered the common parts of a block of flats where the landlord retained control of the common parts and their lighting. The reasoning was based on the fact that in that particular block of flats the common parts provided an essential means of access to the tenant's premises.

In practice, the amendment to section 11 means that the covenant to keep in repair is extended to the structure or exterior of any part of the building in which the landlord has an interest. The covenant to keep the installations in repair and proper working order extends to any installation which directly, or indirectly, serves the dwelling house. Installations must either form part of a building in which the landlord has an interest or which is owned or controlled by the landlord. Common parts liability is more restrictive than section 11(1) liability, in that the landlord will not be required to repair unless the disrepair affects the lessee's enjoyment of the dwelling or the common parts. It is also limited to those common parts which the tenant is entitled to use.

A typical example of common parts liability would be in relation to a common stairwell or lift which a tenant uses for access to his or her flat in a multi-storey block of flats.

What is repair ?

Repairing obligations, whether implied by section 11 or express clause, are just that: obligations to repair. This requires consideration of what is meant by repair. It also implies both that the premises must be kept in repair throughout the tenancy and if necessary must be put into repair first (*Proudfoot v Hart* (1890) 25 QBD 42). The requirement to repair also carries with it a duty to make good or redecorate on the completion of works.

The fact that a social landlord intends to carry out a large-scale programme of works – which may ultimately lead to a general improvement of the stock – does not absolve it from the liability to carry out works to which the tenant has an entitlement on that tenant's complaint or demand. The landlord may therefore be compelled to execute the repairs before the planned programme and it will not be a defence to an application for specific performance that those works could be more economically completed as part of a longer term programme.

Those works which *can* fairly be delayed and included in an estate-wide programme of renovation or improvement can only be identified once it is clear what type of defect the tenant is complaining of and what legal liability arises from it.

If the landlord can show that it has acted reasonably

throughout, especially where a tenant can be shown to have been unreasonable, the court is more likely to find in favour of the landlord.

Repair and improvement

"Repair" does not include improvement. The distinction between repair and improvement is not, however, easy to draw. In order to determine whether works are repairs or improvements it can be helpful to ask questions such as: what was the intention of the parties at the time of the letting? For example, where the intended use is residential, are the premises in a state in which the tenant is able to live in them?

The cost of the repairs as compared to the value of the property as a whole can also be a useful indication. If repairs or alterations are required to the whole or substantially the whole of the structure as opposed to just a part, this may point to improvement rather than repair. If the repairs would produce a building of a wholly different character to that which was the subject of the lease it is more likely that the works will be considered to amount to an improvement.

Whether disrepair exists at a property can firstly be assessed by looking at whether the property's physical condition has deteriorated since its construction. Disrepair is not lack of amenity or efficiency.

The Test

Housing managers responsible for repairs may begin by asking themselves two questions:

1. Is the property in disrepair at all, or is the tenant asking for an improvement?

2. If it is in disrepair, what is the extent of the works

required to repair it and at what point do they become an improvement? (See also the alternative tests approved by the Court of Appeal at pp. 30-31, below).

Until 1980 it was generally accepted that there was a clear dividing line between improvement and repair. Improvement meant the provision of something different in quality to that which was let. This was often accompanied by another proposition: to cure an inherent or design defect meant that the work would be improvement rather than repairs. For example, where a property suffered from damp which was causing disrepair, even if the only way to treat the problem was the insertion of a damp proof course, there was no right to its installation since this would be an "improvement" to the property. The property would not be of the same quality when handed back since it would now have a design feature, i.e. a damp proof course, which it did not previously have.

Examples

In *Ravenseft Properties Ltd v Davstone (Holdings) Ltd* [1980] QB 12 the court dispelled this myth. Here, expansion joints had been omitted from a block of flats because at the time of building the need for them was not recognised, clearly a design defect. As a result of the lack of expansion joints the stone cladding of the property began to fall off. Although putting in such joints would have resulted in an improved structure, the court still found that to put them in would be a repair, not an improvement, since simply to replace the existing cladding would have resulted in a recurrence of the original problem. The

defect amounted to disrepair which required remedying within the repairing covenant, and the
covenant went as far as to require the design fault to
be remedied. However, this case was decided on its
own facts and whether in an individual case the
result will be the same will be a matter of fact and
degree. Of particular relevance in this context is the
cost of the works relative to the value of the property.

In another case, insertion of a chemical damp
proof course in a Victorian house was held to be a
repair rather than an improvement. The original slate
damp proof course had failed. It was stressed that
the question whether this was a repair or an
improvement was a matter of degree (*Elmcroft
Developments Ltd v Tankersley-Sawyer* [1985] 15
HLR 63).

The decision was explained in *Quick v Taff-Ely BC*
[1986] QB 809. The Court of Appeal found that the
insertion of a new damp proof course in the Elmcroft
case "was necessary in order to repair the walls and
although it involved improvement over the previous
ineffective damp proof course, it was held that as a
matter of degree, having regard to the nature and
locality of the property, this did not involve giving
the tenant a different thing from that which was
demised."

It may be that one can distinguish the cases involving
dampness due to absence of a damp proof course from
cases where an old and defective course is replaced, the
latter constituting a repair to something which was previously in existence. It is suggested, however, that it
may not be wise to rely on this distinction. If there is

disrepair to the dwelling, e.g. to the brickwork because of rising damp, it may not matter whether this is caused by the lack of a damp proof course or the fact that an existing one is faulty. There is a disrepair and the question is whether the insertion of the new damp proof course is a repair or an improvement. Generally the cost of insertion will not be great compared to the value of the whole dwelling, and will be the most effective remedy for the disrepair.

In spite of these decisions there remains a division between works of repair and those which extend into works of improvement.

Case report
Easington District Council carried out a major rehabilitation to a council estate which required the removal of the front and rear elevations, removal of the roof and guttering system and stripping of interior fittings. New windows and doors were fitted and the roof replaced and the timber elevations replaced with brickwork costing £10,000. The value to the property was increased by only £8,500. Tenants then claimed compensation for the damage to decorations. They argued that the work came within section 11 of the Landlord and Tenant Act 1985. On these particular facts the court held that the works amounted to improvement. *McDougall v Easington District Council* (1989) 22 HLR 310

Before the issue arises whether the works sought by the tenant or carried out by the landlord amount to a repair or an improvement, it must be shown that there is in the first place disrepair to the dwelling. This question has arisen most starkly in relation to condensation dampness. Dampness is a very common problem encountered with public sector properties and this is often as a result of a design defect. The older properties with metal window frames, poor ventilation and ineffective heating systems notoriously attract condensation dampness, as do those with non-standard designs, using cantilevered rooms and system built uninsulated walls. There is then the secondary problem of mould growth. (On the technical aspects of this problem, see P. Reddin *Dealing with Disrepair*, ch. 3 pp. 45-46, Arden's Housing Library vol. 6, 1996.)

Where there is no actual disrepair it may be argued by the landlord that to remedy the dampness by e.g. changing the window frames would be an improvement and not repair, see below.

Case report
A house let by Taff-Ely Borough Council to Mr Quick was of a certain type of 1970s construction and had always been prone to severe condensation to an extent that it was virtually uninhabitable. The cause of the condensation was a lack of insulation around the concrete window lintels and inadequate heating. There was no evidence of actual lack of repair or damage to either the windows or any part of the structure of the premises. Mr Quick sued for damages resulting from breach of what is now section 11 of the Landlord and Tenant Act 1985. It was held that there was no breach of the landlord's repairing obligation. *Quick v Taff-Ely BC* [1986] QB 809

Where the condensation dampness has resulted in

defective and crumbling plasterwork tenants may successfully argue that the fact of the defective plasterwork means that there is disrepair to the structure or exterior, i.e. the damp has caused disrepair within the terms of section 11 (*Staves v Leeds City Council* (1990) 23 HLR 107). A possible response to such an argument is that plasterwork is not part of the structure or exterior as decided in *Irvine v Moran* (1990) 24 HLR 1 (see above p. 13).

Even where a building is rendered unfit for its intended purpose due to inherent design defects, but those defects do not give rise to physical deterioration, then it will fall outside any repairing obligation (subject to any express covenant to the contrary).

Even though the landlord is not in breach of a repairing obligation because the defect is a design defect causing no disrepair, it may still be the case that the landlord is responsible for causing a statutory nuisance, and therefore liability may ensue under the Environmental Protection Act 1990 (see further below, chapter 6).

Alternative tests

In *McDougall v Easington District Council* (1989) 22 HLR 310 (above p. 28) three different tests to distinguish between repair and improvement were used by the court:
1. whether the alterations go to the whole or substantially the whole of the structure, or are confined to a subsidiary part;
2. whether the effect of the alterations will produce a building of a wholly different character to that which was let;
3. the cost of the works in relation to the prior value of the building and the corresponding effect on the value

and lifespan of the building.

The court held that these tests may be used separately or concurrently. In the *Easington* case the works failed to qualify as repairs on all of them.

Redecoration

The obligation to repair has also been held to include an obligation to make good any consequential damage to decorations: *McGreal v Wake* (1984) 13 HLR 107 (see further p. 116, below).

Notice

Liability under section 11 of the Landlord and Tenant Act 1985 does not arise until the landlord has notice of the disrepair (*O'Brien v Robinson* [1973] AC 912). This does not apply, however, where the disrepair is to parts of the premises over which the landlord retains control. So where the claim is in relation to common parts under section 11(1A), there is no requirement of notice.

The law is not clear whether in the case of an express covenant there must also be notice, even where the tenancy agreement does not require it to be given. The Court of Appeal has held that where there was no requirement of notice in the express repairing covenant, none would be implied. The court did, however, reduce the damages awarded to the tenants because of their failure to inform the landlord (*Minchburn v Peck* (1987) 20 HLR 392). Where an express term is being included in a tenancy agreement, it should always include an obligation to give notice to the landlord, so as to avoid any dispute on this issue.

The requirement to give notice does not mean, however, that it is the tenant who must tell the landlord about the disrepair, nor does it mean that where the tenant does complain he or she has to identify the degree or extent of disrepair. What is needed is sufficient information to alert the landlord that matters must be followed up.

Case report
Ms Jones had been the tenant of Dinefwr Borough Council since 1977. Under her tenancy agreement tenants were requested to address all complaints to the chief housing and environmental health officer, by personal visit, telephone or letter. In 1985 the tenant sought to exercise her right to buy. In connection with this the district valuer inspected the premises in April 1985. His report to the chief executive of the council stated that the valuation reflected certain specified defects.

Prior to this inspection in February 1985 the tenant had been visited by an environmental health officer from the council, who was inspecting the cleanliness of the property. Ms Jones made complaints to the officer about certain items of disrepair. The officer advised her to list them and send the list to the architectural services department. He visited the property again in July 1985 and submitted a report to the council's housing department which included reference to the lack of repair. In February 1986 the council commenced possession proceedings against the tenant for arrears of rent. Ms Jones counterclaimed for disrepair. She paid off the arrears. At trial the judge found that there was disrepair, but that notice had only been given to the council at the second visit of the environmental health officer in July 1985. The Court of Appeal held that as an officer of the council, once items of disrepair had been brought to the attention of the environmental health officer on his first visit in February 1985, notice had been given to the council. Secondly, the district valuer's report contained sufficient information to put the local authority on inquiry about the disrepair. It did not matter that the report was not for the purpose of complaining about the defects. *Dinefwr Borough Council v Jones* (1987) 19 HLR 445

Thus, notice does not need to take a specific form or give particular information, nor does it have to be in writing. It may be given to an agent. In this respect two considerations arise in relation to the contracting out of housing management and building works. Where housing management has been contracted out a local authority will not be able to avoid liability for disrepair by relying on the fact that the notice was not given directly to the contractor. Although in these circumstances councils may prefer that complaints are made to the contractor, the council is still the landlord and in the light of the *Dinefwr* case it does not matter who in the council receives the complaint; notice has still been given.

Notice to an agent

Secondly, there is the question of whether or not notice has been given when complaints are made to workers not directly employed by the landlord. In *Griffin v Pillet* [1926] 1 KB 17 it was held that notice of a defect was sufficient when given to the landlord's builders who were on the premises to deal with another problem. On the basis of this case complaints to workers may well be sufficient. It should certainly be a clause in agreements with any building contractor that all complaints of defects made by tenants will be passed on to the landlord in writing.

The next issue which must be considered is the nature of the notice that must be given. Does the tenant have to specify the detail of what is wrong? The test is simply whether enough information has been provided to put a reasonable person on inquiry as to whether works of repair are needed.

Case report
Mr Sheldon was the tenant of West Bromwich Borough Council. He sought damages against the council arising out of a burst water tank. Prior to the catastrophe the tenant and his wife had made complaints of "water hammering" in the water supply, and there had been some six inspections by plumbers employed by the council. Although this problem did not cause the subsequent burst, one of the plumbers employed by the council had, inspected the tank on a visit. He had found the tank to be discoloured but had not discovered any rust. The county court judge found that the plumber's knowledge of the discolouration of the tank was insufficient notice of the disrepair to the tank to give rise to liability for the burst.

The Court of Appeal, however, reversed this decision. The state of the discolouration of the tank and its age was sufficient to give the council knowledge of the need for repair. They had been put on inquiry about whether works or repair were needed. *Sheldon v West Bromwich Corporation* (1973) 13 HLR 23, CA

"Reasonable time"

There will be no breach of covenant until a "reasonable time" has elapsed since the giving of notice. What is reasonable will depend on the nature and extent of the works required. Thus, the failure to mend a door within a week of being informed of its disrepair was found to be reasonable (*Morris v Liverpool City Council* (1987) 20 HLR 498, CA). One indication of what is a reasonable time may be the response times set by the landlord in any performance indicators used for management purposes. See further P. Reddin *Dealing with Disrepair,* ch. 7 pp. 119-120, Arden's Housing Library vol. 6, 1996. These indicators are, however, target times and a failure to carry out the repair within the target time may not necessarily indicate it has not been carried out within a reasonable time. It is unlikely that a court would strictly equate the two, although they are certainly relevant evidence pointing towards what *might* be a reasonable time.

Summary

Contractual liability is perhaps the most complicated, not to say laborious, area of legal liability for disrepair. That said, there is no escaping the importance of it. It is absolutely fundamental. A tenant's entitlement to repairs depends on the contractual agreement he or she has the benefit of. The written terms may be more extensive than those implied by law but they will never be less so.

The golden rule for dealing with questions of legal liability is to start with the terms of the contract concluded between the parties and only then to go on to consider any other possible avenues open to the tenant.

The following chapter will consider those other non-contractual liabilities. Even when looking to those, however, one must constantly go back to the contract to check whether the agreement makes specific provision which may impact on the extent of liability.

CHAPTER 3

SOCIAL LANDLORD'S NON-CONTRACTUAL LIABILITIES

s4 Defective Premises Act 1972 / Occupiers Liability Act 1957 / s8 Landlord and Tenant Act 1985 / Breach of covenant for quiet enjoyment / s1 Defective Premises Act 1972 / Nuisance / Negligence

On receiving notice, or becoming aware of a defect, a landlord must consider its response. This requires a knowledge of all the avenues open to a tenant in pursuit of his or her legal remedies, whether or not the tenant initially appears to place reliance on them. Once a tenant obtains legal representation it is unlikely that the various alternatives will not be explored. Only by recognising which complaint has merit can a landlord assess the minimum steps required in each given situation. Lawyers are not cheap and once they become involved on a tenant's behalf a social landlord can be quite sure it will not walk away from the experience financially better off. Landlords will be only too familiar with the scenario of a legally aided plaintiff, even if unsuccessful, not being in a position to cover the costs.

In this chapter, therefore, we shall consider the *additional* bases of liability, over and above the contractual liability for disrepair which may arise under the tenancy agreement. In summary these are:

- *s4 Defective Premises Act 1972*

The landlord may be liable for personal injury or damage to possessions of the tenant or a third party where the lease has a repairing covenant or has a right to enter and carry out repairs.

- *Occupiers Liability Act 1957*

The statute imposes duty of care on occupiers of property to their visitors to take reasonable care that the visitor is reasonably safe. The landlord may be the occupier where the property is a hostel occupied by licencees, and also of the common parts of blocks of flats.

- *s8 Landlord and Tenant Act 1985*

This provision implies a contractual term that the property is fit for human habitation. It only applies to properties let at a very low rent.

- *Breach of covenant for quiet enjoyment*

This covenant is implied into all tenancies. Serious disrepair or disruption while works are carried out may constitute a breach of the covenant.

- *s1 Defective Premises Act*

This provision imposes liability on landlords for new building work or conversion works carried out on their behalf. It stipulates that sound and appropriate materials are used, that the work is carried out in a professional and workmanlike manner and that the premises are fit for human habitation on completion.

- *Nuisance*

Interference with the tenant's use or enjoyment of the land by an adjoining occupier is unlawful. This may be the social landlord's responsibility where the problem emanates from common parts or external walls retained in the control of the landlord.

- *Negligence*

A duty of care under common law is imposed on the landlord which may be enforced where there is no contractual or statutory liability. It may be relevant where works have been poorly undertaken and lead to injury, or where the social landlord fails to look after common parts, or where the landlord is the architect or builder of the premises.

s4 Defective Premises Act 1972

Scope

This provision applies where premises are let under a tenancy which imposes on the landlord an express or implied obligation to repair or maintain the premises (whether under section 11 of the Landlord and Tenant Act 1985 or otherwise). Section 4 imposes an additional duty on landlords to take care to ensure that the state of the premises is such that any person who might reasonably be expected to be affected (i.e. not just tenants) by defects in the premises is reasonably safe from personal injury or damage to their property caused by a *relevant defect* in the premises: section 4(1). "Tenancy" has been interpreted to include licences – provided there is a right to occupy.

A defect will be "relevant" if it exists at or after the "material time". This means in the case of tenancies

granted before the commencement date of the Act
(1 January 1974) any time on or after this date. For tenancies granted after 1 January 1974, it means any time
from the commencement of tenancy or if the tenant
moves in prior to the grant, the date of possession.

"Relevant defect"

To be "relevant" the defect must arise from, or continue because of, an act or omission by the landlord
which constitutes (or, if the landlord had notice of the
defect, would have constituted) a failure by the landlord to carry out its obligation to the tenant for the
maintenance or repair of the premises. The duty
applies where there is a defect of which the landlord
knew or ought to have known: section 4(2).

Case report
Mrs Clarke went to visit her sister and brother-in-
law, who were tenants of Taff-Ely Borough Council.
She was intending to help redecorate the living
room. In order to reach the ceiling she stood on a
table. A leg of the table collapsed through a rotten
floor board and she fell and injured her shoulder and
ankle. She sued the council for damages under section 4 of the Defective Premises Act 1972.

Expert evidence was given that knowledge about
the house in question, its type of construction and the
presence of damp, would have made it foreseeable
that rot would occur. If there was rot, floorboards
would give way without warning. The court held the
council was liable on the basis that it ought to have
known about the rot, if it had undertaken a proper

programme of inspection of its dwellings. In other words, the landlord will be liable even if it did not actually know about the defect but should have known about it in all the circumstances. *Clarke v Taff-Ely BC* (1980) 10 HLR 44

Notice

Unlike the requirement for notice under section 11 of the Landlord and Tenant Act 1985, a tenant may be able to establish his or her claim under section 4 of the Defective Premises Act in the absence of express complaint or actual knowledge. This does not mean that a failure to inspect will automatically put the landlord on notice. Rather, where there is a known problem – as was the case in *Clarke* – a reasonable programme of inspection must be undertaken.

Liability under section 4 is limited, however, to damages for personal injury and damage to property. Personal injury will include impairment of a person's physical or mental condition but will not include the more general discomfort and inconvenience typically claimed in an action for breach of the section 11 repairing obligation (see chapter 5, below). Section 4 does not impose an absolute duty to repair but only to take reasonable care. For example, the duty to repair will not arise until the defect is such that it will result in personal injury or damage to property.

The liability under the Defective Premises Act also extends to situations where there is no repairing covenant but the landlord has a right, either express or implied, to enter premises to carry out any types of maintenance or repairs.

Case report

Mrs McCauley was the joint tenant of Bristol City Council. There was a flight of steps leading from the rear garden to the back door and a number of the steps were unstable. Mrs McCauley complained to the council, who denied they were under any liability to repair the steps, since they were not part of the structure and exterior of the house. In October 1984 Mrs McCauley fell on the steps and broke her ankle. She sued the council for damages under section 4 of the Defective Premises Act 1972. The issue which was disputed in the court was whether the council had the implied right to enter and carry out repairs to the steps, even if they were not under any obligation to repair them.

The Court of Appeal held that in order to give "business efficacy" to the lease (see p. 23 above) a term would be implied into the tenancy agreement that the council had the right to enter the premises to carry out repairs to remedy any defects which might expose lawful visitors to the premises (or the tenant herself) to the risk of injury. *McCauley v Bristol City Council* (1991) 23 HLR 586

The social landlord will not, however, have any obligation to the tenant in these circumstances where the defect in the state of the premises arises from or continues because of a failure by the tenant to fulfil his or her express obligations (or obligations implied by statute). (As to the duties of the tenant see further chapter 6, below.) While breach of an express obligation by the tenant is sufficient to defeat an action brought by the tenant based on the resulting defect, under section 4 of the Defective Premises Act the landlord will remain liable to third parties who are injured by the defect. In practice the landlord's only remedy would be to sue the tenant to recover damages for the tenant's breach.

The primary purpose and effect of the Defective Premises Act is to bring third parties – persons who are not signatories to the tenancy agreement – within the protective ambit of repairing obligations. It does not impose on the landlord any liability for failure to carry out works which are not repairs, and cannot therefore be used to deal e.g. with condensation dampness when it is not a disrepair (see above pp. 28-30).

> *Case report*
> Mrs McNerny was the tenant of flat owned by the London Borough of Lambeth. The block was constructed with solid walls and steel window frames. Because of this method of construction the flat suffered from severe condensation dampness. This had consequently caused mould growth and Mrs McNerny and her children had suffered from coughs and colds. She sued the council under section 4 of the Defective Premises Act 1972. The Court of Appeal dismissed the claim. Since there was no liability under the repairing covenant implied by section 11 of the Landlord and Tenant Act, there could be no breach of section 4. *McNerny v Lambeth LBC* (1989) 21 HLR 188

"Premises"

While section 11 refers to "structure and exterior," the Defective Premises Act refers to "premises". In *Smith v Bradford Metropolitan Council* (1982) 4 HLR 86,

Stephenson LJ observed that this was a wider phrase relating to the whole of the premises let (being both land and buildings) and in that case included a raised patio that was in a dangerous condition. Liability under the Defective Premises Act may therefore be somewhat wider than under section 11 of the Landlord and Tenant Act 1985.

However, section 4 of the Defective Premises Act will be confined to the premises let and will not apply, for example, to the common parts of a block of flats.

Occupiers' Liability Act 1957

This Act imposes on occupiers a duty to take reasonable care that visitors will be reasonably safe in using the premises for the purpose for which they have been invited. The occupier will be deemed to be that person who has a sufficient degree of control over the premises to give rise to a duty of care to lawful visitors. (which includes invitees and licensees).

An owner who has parted with possession is not usually an occupier. Consequently, a local authority will not generally be considered an occupier where the dwelling is let on a secure tenancy. It was held, however, in *Greene v Chelsea Borough Council* [1954] 2 QB 127 that a requisitioning authority occupied requisitioned houses which were being lived in by people allocated there by the authority. Thus where rights of occupation are granted which are less than a secure tenancy, e.g. a licence in a hostel, the landlord may still remain in occupation.

This aside, the principal importance of the Act is that it may impose liability for injuries caused by negligence to third parties entering the premises on either the landlord or the tenant.

The statute imposes a duty of care on the landlord towards a tenant in relation to the common parts of a building, i.e. those parts over which the landlord has retained control and thereby occupies them. For example, the landlord can be the occupier of the communal staircase in a multi-storey block of flats and therefore liable to a person injured on the stairs due to the negligence of the landlord (*Fairman v Perpetual Investment Building Society* [1923] AC 74).

s8 Landlord and Tenant Act 1985

This provision implies into all lettings which are at a low rent two further contractual terms: (a) that the premises are fit for human habitation at the date of letting; and (b) that the landlord will keep the premises fit for human habitation for the duration of the letting.

Applicability

Section 8 is, however, very limited in scope and is rarely relevant to public sector lettings. For this section to apply the annual rent (and that is the rent payable at the commencement of the letting, irrespective of the level of the current rent) must be less than:

- (where the date of letting is before 31 July 1923): £40 if the letting is in London; £26 if the letting is in a borough or district council with more than 50,000 people, and £16 in other areas;
- (where the date of letting is on or after 31 July 1923 and before 6 July 1957): £40 if the letting is in London;

£26 if the letting is anywhere else;
• (where the date of letting is on or after 6 July 1957 and before 1 April 1965): £80 if the letting is in London; £52 if the letting is anywhere else;
• (where the date of letting is on or after 1 April 1965): £80 if the letting is in Inner London; £52 if the letting is in Outer London; and £52 if the letting is anywhere else. At such rent levels it is now uncommon to encounter periodic lettings to which the section applies. Where, however, the tenant has been a tenant for a very long period, the provisions may apply.

Breach of covenant for quiet enjoyment

There is a term implied into every tenancy agreement (whether or not the agreement contains an express provision) that the landlord will allow the tenant quietly to enjoy the premises which have been let. The tenant must be permitted to use the premises peacefully and exercise all of his or her rights in relation to it. Examples of breaches of this covenant are wide ranging and have been held to include breach of the repairing obligation. Where a social landlord is in breach of the covenant for quiet enjoyment the tenant will be entitled to damages. The purpose of the award is to put the tenant in the position he or she would have been in had the breach not occurred.

When carrying out major works with tenants still in residence – particularly where the works are to common parts – it will be important to ensure that there is no breach of the tenant's right to quiet enjoyment.

Case report

A property investment company owned a number of blocks of flats, the separate flats being let by the company to individuals. The landlord wanted to upgrade the buildings and began works to construct penthouses in the roofs. These works caused the tenants great interference and inconvenience. In particular, they complained of dust, noise, loss of privacy and deterioration of the common parts. The tenants on the top floor also complained of water penetration which damaged carpets and furniture. The Mira family was one of a number of tenants who sued for breach of the right to quiet enjoyment. The court found that interference with quiet enjoyment included a failure by the landlord to comply with its repairing obligation and the tenants received substantial damages. *Mira v Ayler Square Investments Limited* (1990) 22 HLR 182

s1 Defective Premises Act 1972

This section imposes an obligation on those who carry out work to, or in connection with, the provision of residential accommodation, to use sound and appropriate materials; to carry out the work in a professional and workmanlike manner; and to make sure that the premises are fit for human habitation when the works are completed. The statutory obligation applies to all works commenced after 1 January 1974. It covers not only new building development but also conversion works.

Section 1 applies to architects, builders, surveyors,

electricians and any other persons who carry out work to the premises. It also applies to landlords, including local authorities and housing associations, who engage contractors to do the work.

The duty is owed not only to the person who was provided with the premises but also to anyone who inherits a subsequent legal or equitable interest in the property. The duty is not based in contract but goes somewhat wider and protects the visitors or family of a tenant. Section 3 of the Defective Premises Act extends the obligation to persons who might reasonably be expected to be affected by the defect.

Section 1 of the Act will be relevant where the original building or conversion works are defective, and the tenant or other family or visitors suffer as a consequence.

Case report

Mr Schooling was a property developer who carried out works to a large Edwardian semi-detached house. Following the works Ms Andrews purchased a long lease of the ground floor flat. The lease included the cellar. During the conversion, no works had been carried out to the cellar, which had simply been painted. Soon after moving in Ms Andrew's flat suffered from severe condensation dampness, to such an extent that the flat became unfit for human habitation. The cause of the dampness was the failure to carry out adequate works to the cellar. The Court of Appeal held that section 1 of the Defective Premises Act 1972 could apply to a failure to carry out adequate works, as well as to carrying them out poorly, and made an award of interim damages. *Andrews v Schooling* (1991) 23 HLR 316

Nuisance

Certain kinds of disrepair may also give rise to a claim in nuisance. The liability of landlords for nuisance is dealt with in detail in S. Belgrave *Nuisance and Harassment*, ch. 1, Arden's Housing Library vol. 3, 1995. The focus in this section is on the social housing landlord's liability in private nuisance for disrepair.

The tort (civil injury) of private nuisance is committed where a person commits an act which indirectly causes damage to someone else's land or substantially interferes with the use or enjoyment of the land, and where the injury or interference is not reasonable in the circumstances.

In general, to bring a claim in private nuisance, the person suing must have a proprietary interest in the land affected. A tenant of the local authority may therefore bring such a claim but visitors or lodgers may not. Liability for the nuisance will rest on the person by whose act the nuisance is created or continued. A nuisance may be created or continued by the landlord where premises in its control are in such a state as to interfere with an adjoining property. If the premises comprise a flat which is part of a block of flats and the nuisance emanates from another flat occupied by another tenant, the action in nuisance should properly be brought against that other tenant, not the landlord of the block.

If the social landlord retains part of a building let to a tenant, for example the external rain water pipes, and permits them to fall into a state of disrepair such that water runs down the walls and penetrates the premises of the tenant then the landlord will be liable in nuisance.

Nuisance based on fault?

Liability in nuisance seems to require some element of fault on the part of the person being sued; or at the very least, some knowledge of the defect accompanied by a failure to take steps to remedy it. Where a nuisance is created or continued by a person unlawfully occupying land, the landlord will not be responsible for that person's actions so long as those actions are not expressly or impliedly authorised by the landlord.

Where a nuisance is created due to a landlord's want of repair such that premises become dangerous, the landlord may well be liable whether the danger was known or not (*Wringe v Cohen* [1940] 1 KB 229).

Remedies

Where a private nuisance is established a tenant's remedy will be damages or an injunction or both (see further S. Belgrave *Nuisance and Harassment*, ch. 3, Arden's Housing Library). An injunction will only be appropriate where the condition of premises constitutes a continuing interference with the adjoining property. Damages will be awarded where loss or damage has occurred. If the person claiming damages has been partly responsible for the creation or continuation of the nuisance then the award of damages will be reduced to reflect his or her contribution.

Negligence

The tort of negligence may form the basis of a claim by a tenant against the landlord where premises are in a state of disrepair. The tenant must establish that the landlord owed a duty of care to that tenant and has breached that duty, which resulted in damage which is sufficiently related to the breach. Damage which is too remote from the breach of duty i.e. was not reasonably foreseeable by the wrongdoer, will not be recoverable. Similarly, if the negligent act has not actually caused the damage then the tenant will not recover compensation.

There is no liability, in general, for negligent omission (e.g. a failure to repair as opposed to carrying it out badly) and the courts have been reluctant to impose a duty of care in situations which are already governed by contract and/or statute. It is also still the case that there is generally no liability on the part of the landlord for negligent contractors engaged by the landlord to carry out works, so long as the contractors have not been appointed negligently. A landlord will normally be protected in such a situation by engaging a firm whose reputation is sound and whose expertise is in the required area.

The measure of damages in contract and negligence is different. In a typical disrepair case the award of damages claimed for breach of contract is more likely to be to the tenant's advantage than an award based in negligence. For this reason it is uncommon for an action to be founded in negligence where there is any other contractual breach.

Given the scope of sections 1 and 4 of the Defective Premises Act 1972 (considered above at pp. 47-48 and 39-40 respectively) and the existence of contractual remedies (see pp. 9-10), liability in negligence is likely to be no more than residual. However, it may be used against social housing landlords where works have been undertaken badly as well as in circumstances similar to those in *Liverpool County Council v Irwin* which related to defects to the common parts before the advent of section 11 of the Landlord and Tenant Act 1985 (see above at pp. 22-24). Claims for negligence are particularly likely where the landlord has designed or constructed the premises (see below).

Case report

The plaintiff was a local authority tenant, residing in a flat which had been designed and built by the council. An internal wall in the flat which led from the lounge to the kitchen contained a panel of thin glass and was unprotected in any way. The tenant, in fear for his son's safety, complained to the council about the danger of having such an exposed panel but the council refused to remove it, arguing that it was a standard installation and could not be altered. Subsequently, the tenant tripped while walking past the glass and his hand went through the panel which shattered causing him injury.

The tenant sued the council in negligence for letting a flat which contained a dangerous feature in breach of the duty of care owed to him. The court found the council to be liable. While it was accepted that a landlord of unfurnished premises did not owe any duty of care to a tenant in regard to the state of the premises when they were let, a landlord who had also designed or built the premises owed a duty of care to all persons who might reasonably be affected by the design or construction of the premises. This duty of care was owed to all persons, not just the tenant, who might be affected. The council owed a duty to take reasonable care to ensure that such persons would not suffer injury as a result of faults in the design or construction of the premises. *Rimmer v Liverpool City Council* [1985] QB 1

CHAPTER 4

COMMON TYPES
OF COMPLAINTS

Damp / *Penetrating damp* / *Rising damp* /
Condensation dampness / **Subsidence** /
Roofs / **Asbestos** / **Cockroaches and other
insect infestation**

This chapter looks at the specific problems raised by
some common complaints from tenants and shows
how the principles set out in chapters 2 and 3 may be
applied. The main problems are: damp, subsidence,
roofs, asbestos, cockroaches and other infestations.

Damp

Damp in dwellings may have a variety of causes. The
damp may be penetrating, rising or condensation. See
further P. Reddin *Dealing with Disrepair*, ch. 3 pp. 36-46.

Penetrating damp
Penetrating damp is usually caused by a part of the
building being in a defective state. Often the problem is

found in the walls or the roof but can also be defective guttering or downpipes and windows. In order to establish breach of a repairing covenant it will be necessary to show that there has been damage or deterioration to the dwelling. If the penetration is not caused by damage or deterioration but, for example, is due to a design defect, then the landlord will probably not be liable to repair.

Once, however, it is established that either the damp is caused by deterioration, or the penetrating damp itself has caused some deterioration to the premises, then the covenant to repair will require whatever works are necessary to prevent continuing penetration. The only qualification to this is if the works required are so extensive that they would amount to an improvement as opposed to a repair (see further at pp. 28-29, above).

A common cause of penetrating damp is defective guttering resulting in damp staining to the walls. In this situation the courts will almost always presume that the works required to the guttering will be works of repair within the repairing obligation.

Where the penetration is through a defective roof, it may be sufficient to provide only piecemeal repairs. In the case of *The Trustees of the Dame Margaret Hungerford Charity v Beazeley* (1994) 26 HLR 269 it was decided that patch repairs to a defective roof each time it leaked amounted to sufficient performance of a repairing covenant. The corollary of this decision is that a roof may be in a less than perfect condition but still not be in disrepair for the purposes of the landlord's repairing covenant. If that is so – and the roof in question is watertight and otherwise not failing to fulfil its function – it may be that the landlord will not be held liable simply because the roof is showing signs of ageing and deterioration.

The decision in *Beazley* turned on its own particular facts. However, in another case if a reasonable landlord or surveyor did not consider repeated patch works to be a proper method of undertaking or continuing to treat a defect – in other words if it would be absurd to try to treat a problem in that way – the court is very likely to reach a different decision.

Where the dwelling is a flat, it will also be necessary to consider whether the roof comes within the repairing obligation. For tenancies commencing after 15 January 1989, when section 11 was extended to cover common parts, this should not be problematic (see pp. 22-23, above). For those which commenced prior to this date, in the absence of an express repairing covenant which extends to common parts, the roof may not come within the repairing covenant as it not part of the structure and exterior of dwelling (see pp. 13-14, above).

Rising damp

Rising damp will usually be caused by a defect to, or the absence of, a damp proof course. If the problem is one of a deteriorating course then the problem will have to be remedied by the repair (or replacement if necessary) of the damp proof course.

Where a property has been let without a damp proof course it is often argued that to install a new one would by its very nature amount to an improvement rather than a repair and therefore does not come within the landlord's repairing obligation (see above p. 26). This argument is flawed. Where the absence of a damp proof course has resulted in deterioration to the premises then the landlord will be liable to remedy that deterioration. If the installation of a course is the only proper means of remedying the damage then that is what will be required: *Elmcroft Developments Limited v Tankersley-Sawyer* (1984) 15 HLR 63. In this case it was decided that it was not sufficient to carry out the resultant repairs, for example to perished plaster, without remedying the cause of the disrepair. Here it was a defective damp proof course which needed to be replaced, rather than the complete absence of one which was causing the disrepair.

The principle can, however, be taken further to apply to cases where there is no damp proof course at all. It is not the absence of the course in itself which constitutes a breach of the covenant to repair but the physical damage caused to the premises as a result of it, so that it is necessary to prove that there is actual physical damage caused by the rising damp.

Condensation dampness

For the reasons discussed at pp. 28-29 above, condensation dampness is a very common problem in much local authority stock (see further P. Reddin *Dealing with Disrepair*, ch. 3 pp. 45-46). The problem may not in itself, however, amount to a disrepair falling within an express or implied repairing obligation. Where the condensation has caused considerable damage to internal plasterwork this has been held to be a disrepair (*Staves v Leeds City Council* (1990) 23 HLR 107). A possible response to such an argument is that plasterwork is not part of the structure or exterior as decided in *Irvine v Moran* (1990) 24 HLR 1 (see above p. 13).

Where there can be no recourse to a claim under the repairing covenant, this will also rule out a claim for any damage to property or ill-health caused by the condensation dampness under section 4 of the Defective Premises Act 1972 (see p. 43, above).

Where, however, the condensation is causing mould growth which is "prejudicial to health" the landlord may well be causing a statutory nuisance for which action may be taken under the Environmental Protection Act 1990 (see chapter 6, below). Where the landlord is not a local authority, e.g. a housing association, then it will be the local authority who must take action under the 1990 Act. Where, however, the landlord is the local authority, it will be for the tenant to take action as a "person aggrieved" by the nuisance (see p. 94, below).

Subsidence

It is not uncommon for properties to suffer subsidence damage. Where there has been subsidence it is a usual consequence to have damage to the interior such as cracked floors and plasterwork. In some cases the only effective means of dealing with subsidence is by underpinning. The question then arises, whether the contractual covenant obliges the landlord to carry out the underpinning?

Whether or not underpinning is a repair will depend on the facts of the individual case and the degree of works required, but so far most case law suggests that it will rarely come within the landlord's repairing obligation. However, as with damp proof courses, this may well change in an appropriate case, if it could be shown that underpinning is the only effective form of remedy to the disrepair caused to the dwelling by the subsidence and the cost is not disproportionate to the value of the property. As with penetrating damp, damage occurring as a result of subsidence will usually fall within the covenant to repair unless the works required, looked at in their totality, are so extensive as to fall outside the obligation.

Roofs

Where a roof falls into a state of deterioration due to penetrating damp, for example, the question is not usually whether the defective roof constitutes disrepair but the extent of the works required in order that it be put back into repair. Surveyors can disagree about whether patch repairs are sufficient or complete replacement is necessary. Where alternative methods of repair are contemplated then it is for the landlord, who is bound by the repairing covenant, to decide on the appropriate method. The critical question for the landlord in such a situation is whether continued patch repairs will be sufficient to restore the roof to the condition required by the covenant to keep in repair.

Once the conclusion has been reached on the basis of expert advice that nothing less than complete replacement would suffice, the next step is to consider whether, as a matter of fact and degree, such replacement amounts to a repair and thus comes within the landlord's repairing covenant. Although the answer will depend on all the facts in the individual case it would seem to be arguable that even a completely new roof does not create something different from that which was there before.

In *New England Properties Limited v Portsmouth New Shops Limited* [1993] 1 EGLR 84 the High Court, in finding that replacement was a repair as opposed to an improvement, took into account "... the nature and extent of the defects in design and construction of the roof and the fact that, as a result, it was in imminent danger of collapse; the fact that the comparative cost of merely patching up as opposed to replacing the whole roof was not a substantial difference; ... and the fact that at the end of the day, one still has a roof fulfilling precisely the same function but doing so in such a way which will not involve the occupiers with further disruption by recurring defects."

Asbestos

There is a great deal of concern that many social rented properties contain asbestos. Exposure to asbestos can be very dangerous so it is of the utmost importance that suspected properties are inspected and decisions taken about the future treatment or removal of the substance. Asbestos was particularly used in the building and modernisation of purpose-built blocks of flats and comes in many forms (see P. Reddin *Dealing with Disrepair*, ch. 3 p. 52, 1996). The complex matters surrounding the presence of asbestos and when and how it becomes a danger to occupiers is outside the scope of this book, which will confine itself to the question of asbestos in the context of the landlord's obligation to repair.

The presence of asbestos in itself does not constitute disrepair and therefore the landlord cannot be forced to remove it under the terms of the covenant. Once however the asbestos becomes physically damaged or deteriorated then the landlord will be obliged to have the asbestos encased or removed, since at that point it will be in disrepair, and as it is part of the structure, some action must be taken.

Cockroaches and other insect infestation

Cockroaches or other insect infestation are not of themselves a disrepair and action in relation to such an infestation cannot be taken on the basis of an express or implied repairing covenant. Nor will any term be implied into the tenancy agreement that the landlord ought to take effective action against infestation (see p. 21, above). Nor will there be any liability in negligence for failure to take action. It may, however, be possible that a landlord is liable for an infestation under the law controlling private nuisances (see above p. 49), where the infestation has spread from common parts in the control of the landlord.

Cockroach infestation is a matter which should only be argued on the basis of sound expert evidence. (On infestations generally, see P. Reddin *Dealing with Disrepair*, ch. 3 pp. 49-51, 1996.) There are many aspects to this type of infestation which require background knowledge and experience, e.g. the way in which a premises can become infested, the means of getting rid of cockroaches and so on. It is essential that social landlords faced with claims arising from cockroach infestation obtain a comprehensive expert's report dealing with causation. (On selecting and using experts, see P. Reddin *Dealing with Disrepair*, ch. 9 pp. 142-146, 1996.)

Case report

In *Habinteg Housing Association v James* (also cited on p. 21) the tenant, Mrs James moved into her flat in February 1986 and discovered the flat was infested with cockroaches. Despite itermittent treatment, the infestation was not eradicated until the local authority forced the landlord to block-treat the entire area affected, which included the premises of other tenants on the same estate. From September 1991 onwards the tenant suffered no further infestation.

The landlord took proceedings against the tenant for arrears of rent. She counterclaimed for damages on several bases including breach of an implied term (see p. 21, above for details relating to this claim), nuisance and negligence. The judge dismissed the tenant's counterclaim. In the Court of Appeal it was held:

1. there was no implied term that a landlord should take reasonable care to abate an infestation, even if the block treatment would be the only effective treatment;

2. there was no liability in nuisance because the landlord had not retained any common parts and there was inconclusive evidence about the source of the infestation. Also in this context the court said that the limited reserved rights of entry into the tenanted flats meant that the landlord did not have sufficient control to make it liable for failure to treat an infestation emanating from them;

> **3.** there was no liability in negligence because there is no duty of care on the part of lessors to block-treat infestations where there are no legal means for the lessors to force others on the estate to participate. *Habinteg Housing Association v James* (1994) 27 HLR 299

Social landlords may be held responsible for infestations where the insects are spreading through common parts such as air ducts. Habinteg Housing Association was rather unusual in not retaining control over any common parts in the blocks. It may also be the case that where the landlord takes on responsibility for dealing with the infestation, and then fails to take effective action, there will also be a liability in negligence (see above, pp. 50-51).

> *Case report*
> Mr Sharpe was the tenant of Manchester City Council between 1972 and 1974. The flat suffered extensively from cockroach infestation. The council sought to treat this with DDT, even although use of DDT had been widely disapproved and was considered ineffective. The cockroaches were probably entering the flat through service ducts, but the council failed to treat these. The Court of Appeal held that the infestation amounted to a nuisance, and additionally, that the council's refusal to treat the service ducts and the continued use of DDT amounted to negligence. *Sharpe v Manchester City Council* (1977) 5 HLR 73, CA

Case report

Mrs Jones was the tenant of the London Borough of Wandsworth. She had two children. The family occupied premises in a system-built block with ducted warm air heating. The property was infested with cockroaches. The court found the local authority liable to compensate the tenant for the physical, mental and emotional effects of living in an infested flat. It was held that the scope of the duty to the tenant (whether in nuisance or negligence) involved doing "all that is reasonable to prevent risk of damage and injury to a neighbour's property". The court found that once the local authority had assumed responsibility for the treatment of the infestation it took much too long to devise and implement a block treatment programme. The local authority argued that it was the ducting on the estate which provided a means of access for the cockroaches but that the cockroaches were not emanating from the common parts. This was rejected by the county court. *Clark v London Borough of Wandsworth*, June 1994, *Legal Action*

CHAPTER 5

TENANT'S REMEDIES

Specific performance and injunctions / *Interim injunctions* / *Limits to specific performance* / *Resisting the application* / *Evidence and agreeing the works* / *Failure to carry out the works* / **Damages** / *Special damages* / *General damages* / *Interest* / **Limitation periods** / *Breach of contract* / *Negligence* / **Duty to mitigate** / **Direct action** / *Set-off against rent* / *Set-off and counterclaims* / *Using rent to pay for repairs* / **Right to repair (secure tenants)** / *"Qualifying repairs"* / *Reporting repairs* / *"Prescribed periods"* / **Appointment of a receiver or manager**

Where all the landlord's intentions have failed to avoid a confrontation, the tenant will seek to get satisfaction through the courts, or otherwise! There is a number of things which an aggrieved tenant may do: some of these have the backing of the courts; others are purely practical or tactical.

Faced with tenant action the landlord must assess the likelihood of success, and decide whether the fight is worth the time and expense necessarily involved.

Disrepair is one area of the law where principle costs and the fact that a social landlord is charged with providing subsidised housing from increasingly constricted budgets is not an excuse at law for inaction in an individual case.

One claim which succeeds may disrupt, if not frustrate altogether, a planned programme of works scheduled for the longer term. A social landlord wants to make best use of its resources and this may depend on the landlord pre-empting court action by carrying out those works which it is likely that the court will order, retaining other works within its planned programme.

To achieve this fine balance, a landlord needs to appreciate the scope of the tenant's remedies in each particular case. Even if the matter ends up in the courts, all is not necessarily lost and the landlord may successfully oppose a tenant's application. This chapter sets out the most common remedies available to tenants and the possible responses available to a social landlord.

The principal remedies which a tenant is likely to seek from a social landlord alleged to be in breach of repairing obligations are: specific performance (including mandatory injunction), i.e. ordering the work to be done; and damages, i.e. monetary compensation.

Specific performance and injunctions

This remedy means that the court can order the social landlord to comply with its repairing obligations by doing the works. The court has specific power under section 17 of the Landlord and Tenant Act 1985 to order works to be done (*Gordon v Selico* (1986) 18 HLR 219).

Section 17 provides that where a tenant alleges in the course of proceedings a breach of the repairing obligation relating to any part of the premises containing the dwelling, the court may order specific performance of that repairing obligation. This means that a landlord can be compelled to carry out works even where the breach does not relate to the premises let to the tenant but, for example, to common parts.

Specific performance and injunctions can be awarded in the small claims court. In appropriate cases, i.e. where the value of the damages is below the small claims limit (currently £3,000) the case should be brought in that court (*Joyce v Liverpool City Council* (1995) 27 HLR 548).

Interim injunctions

These are extremely popular with tenants as the court can compel the landlord to remedy those problems of which a tenant complains. For social landlords, they can prove very costly and inconvenient. A court may order the landlord to accord priority to an individual tenant at the expense of a wide ranging programme of works aimed at benefitting all of the tenants on a particular estate.

In itself, however, this is not sufficient reason to refuse the order if the tenant can satisfy the court that otherwise they are entitled to have the work done pending a full court hearing.

It is essential in this context that the landlord is seen to be acting reasonably. The grant or refusal of an interim injunction is within the judge's discretion – it is an equitable remedy – the judge will weigh up the merits of the case in deciding whether to order this relief or – which may be more important – just *how much* of it to order. Appendix I contains a checklist which, if followed, may assist in establishing to the court that the landlord has done everything reasonably within its power.

The test for obtaining an interim injunction is strict yet social landlords and housing managers will be only too aware of how ready the courts are to grant this relief. Whenever a social landlord is brought to court on such an application it is worth reminding the judge just how much the tenant must establish before the application is granted. The following sets out the legal framework for these applications and some of the responses open to the landlord to avoid them.

The test

If there is disrepair which immediately threatens damage to health or property, an interim injunction forcing the landlord to do urgent works may be sought by the tenant before the case goes to trial. The county court can grant such an injunction even where there is no claim for damages: section 38 (as substituted) of the County Courts Act 1984.

An interim order requiring the landlord to carry out works (a mandatory injunction) should only be made by the court where there is a real risk to health and safety (*Parker v London Borough of Camden* [1986] Ch 162). Such orders should be granted only in exceptional circumstances (*Locabail International Finance Ltd v Agroexport* [1986] 1 All ER 901).

Limits to specific performance

Specific performance is a discretionary remedy and a

tenant seeking to enforce a repairing obligation in this way must establish that:
- it is just and equitable in all the circumstances for specific performance to be granted;
- the works required to be carried out can be adequately itemised;
- damages would not be an adequate remedy.

Specific performance is the usual remedy sought by tenants alleging breach of repairing obligation. Often an order requiring works to be done will prove extremely costly to social housing landlords. Inability to comply with an order for specific performance for financial reasons, however, will not normally be a defence to an action. (On making a case for deferring works for finalised reasons, see P. Reddin *Dealing with Disrepair*, ch. 7 pp. 127-128.)

Resisting the application

Despite this, a landlord does have some defences with which to resist an order for specific performance. First of all, the claim can be defended where a tenant delays in bringing proceedings for an unreasonable length of time. A tenant is required to act as promptly as circumstances permit. A court should not order that works be carried out if there would be no point to the exercise. This would be the case for example, where the dwelling is to be demolished or completely renovated in the near future and the tenants are to move in any event. Thirdly, an order should not be made where it would be impossible to carry out the proposed works. For example where a tenant is seeking an order for specific performance of the repairing obligation and because of an intervening act before the date of the final hearing which was due to the fault of the tenant such as fire damage, the landlord will be unable to do the required works without first reinstating the premises. Since the landlord is not liable for such reinstatement it will be impossible to order the works to be carried out.

Social landlords are increasingly faced with court orders requiring them to do expensive works for which they simply do not have adequate funding. Short of central government dipping its hand into the nation's pocket (or the national lottery fund) and providing the additional money this problem is not going to go away. Unfortunately, there is no easy answer save for social landlords to practice more preventative measures and pre-empt unnecessary actions against them.

The only way to achieve this is to adopt a tightly regulated programme of responses, and to stay on top of the law.

Evidence and agreeing the works

Where a social landlord faces a claim for specific performance, good evidence will be critical. It is recommended that an inspection is carried out quickly by a qualified surveyor armed with a copy of the tenant's schedule of works. (See P. Reddin *Dealing with Disrepair*, ch. 9 pp. 138-142 on selecting and using experts.) The surveyor can then agree or disagree that the works need to be done, and if the works are agreed the surveyor may comment on the preferred method or time required. Often it will be possible to arrange a joint inspection with the tenant's expert and this will save court time and costs.

If the landlord's surveyor agrees that the works are required and the landlord accepts liability for them, then these works should be undertaken speedily to avoid increasing any claim for damages which may also be outstanding.

Failure to carry out the works

Sometimes social landlords fail to comply with injunctions or consent orders regarding the carrying out of works. A failure to comply with a court order leaves the landlord open to an action for contempt, under which the court may fine or imprison. Once the date set in the order to carry out the works has passed the tenant may apply for committal to prison, and this can be directed at an officer of the social landlord. In some cases tenants have sought committal against the director of housing of local authorities who have failed to carry out works ordered by the court.

The detailed procedure for committal is laid down in Order 29 of the County Court Rules 1981. A copy of the judgment or order must be served on the director or other officer of the body against whom the committal is sought. The order must include what is known as a penal notice which warns of the consequences of failure to comply. Although a particular name does not have to be included in the penal notice, in *R v Wandsworth County Court, ex p. Munn* (1994) 26 HLR 697 it was held that a name could be included on either the application of the tenant or with the consent of the landlord. In this case the tenant sought to have the director of housing for the London Borough of Lambeth named.

The organisation may wish to have the attention of the responsible officer called to his or her potential liability; or, if the court is minded to name someone on the tenant's application – regardless of the landlord's consent – the landlord may prefer to volunteer the correct name.

Although there have been no reported cases where a director of housing has actually been sent to prison, there have been a number of times where judges have come close to making such an order. Housing managers should seek to avoid such embarrassment and attendant bad publicity by ensuring early compliance with any court orders to carry out works. If a landlord cannot comply within the time set by the court for unavoidable reasons then the landlord should apply to the court before expiry of the time limit for a variation of the order to provide for extra time.

Damages

This is the ultimate penalty for failure to comply with repairing obligations and the force of the penalty is beginning to hit home. One only has to read the judgments in the Housing Law Reports to see how levels of damages awards are sky rocketing (see Appendix II).

It is the tenant's adviser's job to ensure that the court sets the level of compensation as high as possible. This does not mean that social landlords need put their hands in the air and submit to the full force of the court's disfavour (although in some cases throwing in the towel early, accompanied by a realistic offer of settlement, may well save money in the long term) instead it can argue that the appropriate test for damages should not give rise to large windfall gains, and present its own more appropriate comparables.

Where a tenant successfully sues for breach of a

repairing obligation the damages awarded are damages in contract. The measure of damages will be governed by the principles of the common law on assessment of contractual damages. The underlying principle is that such damages are designed to put the party who has suffered the breach in the same position as if there had been no breach. Generally the tenant will be put in the position he or she would have been in had the breach not occurred, by calculating the diminution in the value of the premises (*Calabar Properties v Stitcher* [1984] 1 WLR 287).

Damages will be calculated from the date on which the social landlord is in breach of covenant. A landlord will not be in breach of the repairing covenant contained in section 11 of the Landlord and Tenant Act 1985 until a reasonable time has elapsed from the giving of notice. Therefore there will be a period between the occurrence of the defect and the carrying out of works which will not be recoverable in damages so long as the social landlord does not delay unreasonably in the carrying out of the works (see p. 31 above).

Compensation in damages can be of two types – special damages and general damages.

Special damages
Special damages are the amounts awarded by the court for specific and quantifiable losses e.g. damaged clothes, damaged furniture and decorations, extra heating bills, loss of earnings, cost of eating out (e.g. if food storage or cooking facilities have been damaged). The amount awarded for items damaged beyond repair is their second-hand value. If the disrepair renders the premises uninhabitable, the tenant may recover in

damages the cost of taking alternative accommodation from the date when the premises could no longer be occupied to the date of assessment or repair.

The existence and extent of the matters giving rise to special damages will naturally depend on the circumstances of each case. A tenant must formally plead the special damages he or she is claiming and each item of loss must be proved.

General damages

General damages are the amount assessed by the court for losses which do not represent a specific sum but which relate to the loss of value of the tenancy to the tenant. What this means is the difference between the value of living in the premises in their defective condition and the value of living in premises in the condition they should have been in had the landlord not failed to repair them.

The court will usually assess damages by taking a proportion of the rent and/or an amount to represent the additional inconvenience and distress (if there was any) caused by the disrepair. Tenants may also recover general damages for injury to health. If the injury alleged is more than just coughs and colds then the tenant must plead this as they would a personal injury claim (in other words there must be a proper medical report annexed to the Particulars of Claim). Where this requirement is not complied with, it may be possible to have that element of the claim struck out or disallowed.

The purpose of awarding general damages is not "to punish the landlords but, so far as money can, to restore the tenant to the position he would have been in had there been no breach." (Griffiths LJ in *Calabar*

Properties). The courts, however, have not adopted one set formula for the assessment of general damages. Each case is looked at on an individual basis and any assessment takes account of the particular circumstances of the case. Some awards are made as a global figure which calculates a sum on an annual basis taking into account inconvenience, distress and loss of value e.g. the unpleasantness of living in a dilapadated house (*Lubren v London Borough of Lambeth* (1987) see p. 144, below). Other awards are broken down into two separate amounts: (i) for the loss in value assessed as a discount or rebate on the rent; and (ii) for inconvenience and injury, distress and injury to health (*Sturolson & Co v Mauroux* (1988) see p. 145, below). Adopting this two-pronged approach may result in the tenant being compensated twice for the same element of loss.

While the usual method will be to take a reduction in the rent, where rent levels are low the court is not confined by this figure.

Case report
Miss De Marney, a private tenant living in a one-bedroomed flat and paying a registered rent of £8 per week, claimed damages for disrepair. The claim encompassed a failure to repair the hot water heater with the result that there had been no hot water for five years. The flat was permeated with dampness, there were broken windows, cracks in the walls, holes in the roof and dangerous wiring and cables. The premises were described by the court as "really quite intolerable". Damages were assessed on the basis of a weekly sum for the period during which the property

was in disrepair. This was to represent the diminution in value to the tenancy, including the general inconvenience and distress of living in such conditions, of £30 a week. The court did not confine itself to the level of rent actually paid by the tenant, and it would seem, did not even use the rent recoverable as a guide to assessing the difference in value. The Court of Appeal said that the lower court "in seeking to assess a sum to compensate fairly for discomfort and loss of enjoyment was right and . . . was not in error in failing to take account of the rent as a prima facie indication of the level of any proper award." *Personal Representatives of Chiodi v de Marney* (1988) 21 HLR 6

Where there is severe disrepair, damages can run into thousands of pounds.

Case report
Ms McLarty was a secure tenant and single woman in her fifties. The premises were described as being in a state of serious disrepair. The whole of the flat had been damp and wet for three years. A burst water pipe under the kitchen floor made the kitchen and bathroom floors constantly saturated with water to such an extent that she had to wear wellington boots in these rooms. There was also water running down the walls from the flat above with the result that the electric wiring was dangerous. Ms McLarty suffered two electric shocks from the electric sockets. The back door of the premises would not shut properly. As a result of all of this she developed insomnia. The court, on deciding the level of general damages for

inconvenience, discomfort and distress said "...the facts of this case warrant an assessment in the highest bracket of damages". Admitting that the award of damages was not an exact science, the court awarded £4,000 under this heading. The court also found that the conditions exacerbated the tenant's rheumatism and eczema and awarded a further £1,900 for injury to health. *McLarty v London Borough of Islington* October 1992 *Legal Action*

Case report
Mr Yilmaz lived with his wife and two children in a flat owned by the London Borough of Hackney. The flat had extensive general disrepair for a period of five years and partly as a result of that disrepair all the occupiers had suffered anxiety and depression. The tenant received £5,000 general damages for inconvenience, and a further £1,000 to each child and £500 to each of the parents for the psychiatric illness. *Yilmaz v London Borough of Hackney* March 1995 *Legal Action*

Damages for redecoration

A tenant can claim (as part of damages for disrepair) the cost of redecoration carried out in default of the landlord's obligation to make good after repairs are actually carried out. (See also P. Reddin *Dealing with Disrepair*, ch. 8 pp. 132-133.) While, in general, damages should not put the tenant in a better position than before the breach of the repairing covenant, damages will not be disallowed because the new decorations are giving the tenant a higher standard than prior to the works, if this is the only way that the decorations can be carried out.

Case report
Ms McGreal was a private sector tenant. The local authority served a repairs notice on her landlord in November 1979. When he failed to carry out the repairs the authority did the works themselves. They did not, however, redecorate the property. Ms McGreal claimed for the costs of redecoration and the Court of Appeal allowed her claim, notwithstanding that the redecorations were an improvement to the previous state of the property. *McGreal v Wake* (1984) 13 HLR 107.

Further examples of awards of general damages are set out in Appendix II.

Interest

Claims for damages frequently include a claim for interest on the amount of the award pursuant to section 69 of the County Courts Act 1984. This may be a general claim for interest on the whole of the award, however, interest is only payable on special damages, not general damages. The logic behind this is that it is only appropriate to award interest on claims for economic loss, in other words, to compensate for money which the tenant would have had. A claim for economic loss can properly include damage to goods, furniture and fittings etc. (otherwise referred to as chattels).

It does not include damages for inconvenience, distress and discomfort, as so commonly pleaded in disrepair claims.

Limitation periods

There is a three-year limitation period for personal injury actions and a six-year period in all other cases. In practice, a social landlord dealing with an allegation of injury to health must always plead the Limitation Act 1980 which limits damages recoverable, e.g. for personal injury to those incurred in the three years previous to the issue of proceedings. The effect of the Limitation Act may be that there is no cause of action in respect of the injury if brought after three years from the date of the injury. Damages which are awarded will also be limited to the three year period prior to the issue of proceedings. The key date for the purpose of limitation is the date when the cause of action accrues.

Breach of contract

For claims based on breach of the contractual obligation to repair, the date of the breach of the obligation (in other words following notice of the disrepair and a reasonable period to remedy it) is the date from which the landlord may be liable. If repairs are not then carried out the cause of action is a continuing one but the recovery of damages will be limited to the circumstances of the six years preceding the issue of proceedings.

Negligence

For claims based in negligence the cause of action accrues at the date of the negligent act. Recovery of damages will be limited to six years preceding the issue of proceedings. Where there is a personal injury the limitation period will begin to run from the date of the injury. This will be the case even if the cause of the injury, for example the letting of premises in a defective state, was many months or years before. Claims arising under section 1 of the Defective Premises Act 1972 will also be subject to the six year limitation period. The date from which the cause of action normally accrues, however, will be the date on which the building or – works carried out to it – was completed.

Duty to mitigate

It is a general principle that the plaintiff is under a duty to mitigate his or her loss, i.e. the tenant is expected to take such steps as are reasonable (e.g. minor or temporary measures) to limit any loss caused by disrepair. For example if there is a leak from the bathroom to the lounge below, a tenant would be expected to at least place a bucket under the leak to prevent soaking of carpets and floors. Also, where the tenant has delayed to a great extent in giving notice of the defect to the landlord with the result that the damage is much more severe than it would have been, the tenant will have his or her compensation reduced to represent the failure to mitigate loss.

Case report
The tenant complained of dampness, reporting it to his landlord in March 1984. During that year some minor repairs were carried out to the roof. It was not however, made watertight by this work nor was it until April 1986, when further works were carried out. The Court of Appeal held that while in that case

(due to the terms of the lease) the repairing obligation was not an obligation to repair on notice, the tenant was under a duty to mitigate by giving notice of the disrepair at an early stage, and failure to do so went counter to the amount of damage, in particular for discomfort and inconvenience, since the tenant could have improved his position by giving notice to the landlord.

In giving judgment Dillon LJ stated "There is, however, a possibility that if the defendant had badgered at a yet earlier date, the final result would have been achieved a bit sooner..." The trial judge had awarded damages of £1,050 including £800 general damages; on appeal the latter was reduced to £700 on the basis that the tenant's loss would have been less extensive if he had "badgered" the landlord at an earlier date. *Minchburn v Peck* (1987) 20 HLR 392

Whether it would have been reasonable to expect the tenant to take specific steps to limit the damage will depend on the circumstances of the case and of the particular tenant. For example it may be reasonable to expect a young fit person to take simple steps to remedy a leak while it may not be reasonable to expect an elderly or disabled person to take the very limited steps to control flooding by placing buckets under a leak.

Often in cases of disrepair a tenant will claim damages for the unpleasantness and inconvenience of living in the premises while works are being carried out. Where the works to be carried out are major ones which will considerably interfere with the tenant's occupation, a landlord may be better advised to offer temporary accommodation (if available) for the duration of the works. If this offer of accommodation is unreasonably refused it may be argued that the tenant has failed to mitigate his or her loss and will be unable to recover damages for the trouble of living through the works.

Direct action

Set-off against rent

Where a tenant simply withholds rent, instead of seeking legal redress, he or she will be open to eviction for non-payment of rent. Many housing managers will be familiar with cases of tenants withholding rent as a protest against the landlord's failure to repair. This is not strictly a legally permissible remedy (see, however, further below at p. 84).

Housing managers, however, will be aware of the courts' increasing acceptance of this practice. Where, for example, possession is being sought and the court must be satisfied that it is reasonable to make an order courts rarely find it reasonable where the arrears are because the tenant is living in squalor and had refused to pay while those conditions continued.

The courts show particular tolerance for those tenants who withhold rent but put it to one side until the outcome of the dispute over repairs. Where a landlord is considering taking proceedings against a tenant for non-payment of rent it is often worth considering the likelihood of a counterclaim for damages which may greatly exceed the claim for rent.

Set-off and counterclaims

An unascertained claim in damages for breach of the landlord's repairing obligation can be set-off against arrears of rent (*British Anzani v International Marine* [1979] 2 All ER 1063). So if possession proceedings are brought against the tenant and the tenant counterclaims for damages for disrepair, the damages may be set-off against the claim for rent arrears and extinguish the landlord's claim, thus leaving no rent lawfully due. Where damages extinguish the amount of the rent arrears, the tenant's equitable set-off will give the tenant a complete defence to a possession action. This will be the case even where the tenant has neither carried out the works nor instructed a contractor to do the works. The set-off is a claim for general damages and therefore may go beyond the actual cost of any works. This remedy is based on the proposition that it would be inequitable (i.e. unfair) for the landlord to recover the rent claimed. For that reason the tenant must establish (a) that it would be inequitable – not usually a problem for breach of a contractual obligation – and (b) that the set-off arises under the tenancy agreement. A tenant wishing to raise a set-off must have formally pleaded it in the defence to a possession action and will usually have raised it as a counterclaim.

Even if the damages award does not totally extinguish the arrears, the court may refuse to make an outright order for possession on the basis that the court is not satisfied that it would be reasonable to do so. It has been held by the Court of Appeal that where the level of rent arrears on which possession proceedings have been founded is less than the damages on the counterclaim for disrepair, then it will not be reasonable for the court to order possession (*Televantos v McCulloch* (1990) see p. 147, below).

There may be instances, however, where the claim fails completely, or in large measure. In these circumstances, unless the tenant can provide assurances that the arrears can be cleared by other means, an outright order is appropriate.

Case report

Mr Stewart was the tenant of the London Borough of Haringey. He had arrears of rent of £1,200 and in March 1989 possession proceedings were commenced against him. He eventually defended the action and counterclaimed for breach of the repairing covenant. For the next 12 months, until the case came to trial in July 1990, Mr Stewart failed to pay his rent on a regular basis. The case was adjourned on several occasions, and in the meantime the Mr Stewart was placed in custody on a criminal charge.

The counterclaim was dismissed and the judge made an outright order for possession, as the tenant was unable to make an offer to clear the arrears. The Court of Appeal in upholding this decision stated that a tenant who fails in a counterclaim for disrepair must equip him or herself to make an immediate or early provision for the discharge of outstanding arrears or accept the consequences. Given that there were no proposals to discharge the arrears the judge was not obliged to consider imposing a suspended possession order. *London Borough of Haringey v Stewart* (1991) 23 HLR 557

Using rent to pay for repairs

Using rent to pay for repairs is only a legally permissible course of action for tenants in very limited circumstances. Where a landlord is in clear breach of repairing obligations, it is now well established that tenants may do works themselves or employ a contractor and deduct the expense from future rent. In other words where a tenant has spent his or her own money in carrying out the works and then recoups it from the rent he or she is acting within the law (*Lee-Parker v Izzet* [1971] 1 WLR 1688).

Such a claim will be successful only if the tenant has:
1. informed the landlord of his or her intention to do so
2. allowed a further period for the landlord to do the works
3. obtained three estimates, sent copies to the landlord and given a final warning
4. employed a builder at the cheapest rate
5. sent a copy of the invoice to the landlord and asked for reimbursement
6. recouped the cost of the repairs from rent (only if no money is forthcoming).

In these circumstances the tenant is not in arrears since the rent is no longer legally due. This is different from the right to set-off against rent discussed above, but will also provide a complete defence to an action for the arrears. This right to recoup from future rent will be limited to the actual cost of the works. It does not include an amount for unascertained general damages for breach of the covenant to repair.

It has been argued that where such a course of action is reasonably available to a tenant then failure to utilise the remedy should result in a damages award as the tenant has failed to mitigate his or her loss. This point has not yet been finally determined by the courts but it is suggested that it would not be wise to rely upon it. This could be construed, in substance, as an attempt to shift the burden of organising and effecting repairs that are the landlord's responsibility onto the tenant.

Right to repair (secure tenants)

The Secretary of State has power to make regulations entitling secure tenants to have qualifying repairs carried out at the landlord's expense in dwelling-houses of which they are secure tenants, and for compensation for failure to repair within the prescribed period (section 121 of the Leasehold Reform, Housing and Urban Development Act 1993 whereby a new section 96 has been substituted in the Housing Act 1985).

The new right to repair scheme for secure council tenants (i.e. it is not applicable to other secure tenants e.g. of housing associations) came into force on 1 April 1994 under the Secure Tenants of Local Housing Authorities (Right to Repair) Regulations 1994. The entitlement to repairs and compensation does not apply where the landlord has fewer than 100 dwelling-houses let to secure tenants on the day it receives an application to have repairs carried out. The Regulations also cease to apply if the tenant fails to provide details of the arrangements for the contractor to obtain access or to provide access for an inspection to be carried out.

"Qualifying repairs"

The Regulations only apply to qualifying repairs which are listed as:

- total loss of electric power
- partial loss of electric power
- unsafe power or lighting socket, or electrical fitting
- total loss of water supply
- partial loss of water supply
- total or partial loss of gas supply
- blocked flue to open fire or boiler
- total or partial loss of space or water heating
- blocked, or lack of, foul drain, soil stack or (where there is no other working toilet in the dwelling-house) toilet pan
- toilet not flushing (where there is no other toilet in the dwelling-house)
- blocked sink, bath or basin
- tap which cannot be turned on or off
- leaking from water or heating pipe, tank or cistern
- leaking roof
- insecure external window, door or lock
- loose or detached bannister or hand rail
- rotten timber flooring or stair tread
- door entryphone not working
- mechanical extractor fan in internal kitchen or bathroom not working.

Reporting repairs

The greatest impact of this scheme is likely to be seen with councils' repair reporting arrangements. The effect of the Regulations is that when a tenant reports a defect the council must inspect forthwith (if it is considered that an inspection is required), or issue the tenant with a notice in writing. The notice must either set out that an order has been placed with a contractor to carry out the repair (and enclose a copy of that order), or explain that the repair is not within the scheme and why it is not. The tenant must also be provided with a clear explanation of the terms of the scheme. From 1 April 1994 therefore every tenant who reports a defect should have a written record of that complaint and is therefore on notice of it. In the light of this every local authority should revise their logging of complaints procedure. Where a tenant brings proceedings for disrepair after the relevant date but there is no record of the complaint, it may be accepted as evidence that the alleged complaint was not made, provided the court accepts the accuracy of the landlord's procedure for logging complaints.

"Prescribed periods"

The Regulations also provide for "prescribed periods" within which specified types of repair should be completed. These should be adhered to by the local authority where at all possible, as tenants in future are likely to use the prescribed periods as an indication of what is a reasonable period for the purposes of section 11 of the Landlord and Tenant Act 1985.

As regards compensation under the Regulations, a tenant is entitled to a specified sum if the qualifying repair is not carried out within the prescribed period. As can be seen from this list of works, on the whole the repairs to which the scheme applies do not involve major structural problems, although from the tenant's point of view they will be urgent. The level of compensation has been set fairly low, being the lower of £50 or

£10 per day for each day past the prescribed period for completing the works.

Appointment of a receiver or manager

Section 37 of the Supreme Court Act 1981 gives the High Court power to "appoint a receiver in all cases in which it appears to the court to be just and convenient to do so". In such a case the county court also has power to appoint a receiver (*Yorston & Yorston v Crewfield Ltd and Others* July 1985 *Legal Action*). This procedure may be used against certain types of social landlord where there is persistent neglect of repair and maintenance obligations. In *Parker v London Borough of Camden* [1985] 2 All ER 141 it was held that section 37 does not apply for the benefit of tenants of local authorities. It will however be exercisable against other social landlords such as housing associations.

In deciding whether it is just and equitable to appoint a receiver the court will look to all the circumstances of the case. In particular the court will consider: the works required; the likelihood of them being carried out by the landlord; the obligation to carry out those works; and the necessity of them being done. Where a receiver is appointed the landlord no longer has the right to receive rent. If the court has also empowered the receiver with powers of management then the receiver may use the rent received to pay for the cost of the works.

The receiver/manager will be appointed to deal with a specific property (and where there are two or more flats contained in a single block the power of the court is now contained in the Landlord and Tenant Act 1987). If this Act applies then the general equitable jurisdiction derived from section 37 of the Supreme Court Act is excluded. The Landlord and Tenant Act 1987 expressly does not apply to public bodies (which includes housing associations and local authorities) and therefore section 37 is the relevant provision, if it is applicable.

CHAPTER 6

PUBLIC HEALTH DUTIES

Environmental Protection Act 1990 /
*Statutory nuisance / Local authority
duty to residents / Action by tenants /
Procedure / Compensation orders /
Appeals / Costs / Contingency fees /*
Other public health provisions /
*Sanitary facilities / Drains and sewers /
Vermin / Fire precautions and dilapidation*

While most of this book is concerned with the liability of the landlord and tenant towards each other for repair, it may be that in some circumstances action may be taken through public health legislation. Part III of the Environmental Protection Act 1990 governs statutory nuisances. While enforcement of the legislation is primarily undertaken by local authorities, it is also possible in some circumstances for an affected tenant to take action, providing an additional remedy for the tenant. Social landlords, particularly local authorities, may well find themselves having to defend such actions.

These actions are criminal in nature and can be founded on defects to property which do not come within the express or implied repairing obligation. A prime example is dampness caused by condensation which is a design defect.

Environmental Protection Act 1990

Part III of the Act makes provision for service by local authorities of abatement notices (section 80) and for the prosecution of those in default (section 81). Section 82 makes provision for prosecution by individuals "aggrieved" by a statutory nuisance. (See also generally S. Belgrave *Nuisance and Harrassment*, ch. 1, Arden's Housing Library vol. 3, 1995).

Statutory nuisance

Section 79 sets out a number of circumstances which amount to a statutory nuisance. These include (most relevantly to disrepair) where "any premises are in such a state as to be prejudicial to health or a nuisance" (section 79(1)(a)). The term "any premises" includes both the social rented and private sector housing. There is no requirement that the premises are occupied at the time. It is important to remember that it is the effect of the defects or the state of the premises as a whole which gives rise to the statutory nuisance.

Premises may be "in such a state" even though the origin of the nuisance is outside the premises e.g. where dampness seeps in. The premises must also be

"...prejudicial to health or a nuisance..." These are alternate tests and satisfaction of one limb is sufficient.

Prejudicial to health
Prejudicial to health is defined as "injurious or likely to cause injury to health" (section 79(7)). This includes actual and potential ill health, and will be sustained where premises are so defective as to cause actual or potential detriment to the health of occupiers. Health includes physical and mental health. Mere interference with comfort is not enough.

The threat to health must be posed by the very existence of the alleged statutory nuisance, not simply by the presence of dangerous objects such as glass fragments. In *Coventry City Council v Cartwright* [1975] 1 WLR 845 it was held that the accumulation of inert builders' rubble did not constitute a statutory nuisance as it was not likely to cause disease even though the rubbish contained potentially hazardous matter such as glass. The court found that had the rubbish contained toxic substances then it would have come within the definition and been a statutory nuisance. Organic waste left to rot is certainly prejudicial to health.

What is prejudicial to health is essentially a matter of expert evidence for doctors and environmental health officers. It is absolutely essential that any social landlord faced with a problem of premises allegedly being prejudicial to health seeks expert advice, which must then be presented to the court in the form of an expert's report.

The court will not substitute its views for those of a qualified person (unless the evidence is disbelieved). Therefore where a social landlord is facing an action in statutory nuisance backed by expert evidence, and the landlord cannot offer contrary evidence, a defence will not succeed on the argument that the nuisance complained of is not prejudicial to health.

Nuisance

The alleged nuisance can be either a public nuisance which affects the comfort or quality of life of the public generally, or a private nuisance where the actions of the owner or occupier of a property interferes with the use and enjoyment of a neighbouring property.

Thus to be a nuisance the condition complained of must either arise on one property and interfere with the use and enjoyment of an adjoining property for a substantial period (private nuisance), or arise on one property and affect the comfort and quality of life of members of the public (public nuisance) (*National Coal Board v Neath Borough Council* [1976] 1 WLR 543).

Local authority duty to residents

Under section 79 of the 1990 Act it is the duty of every local authority to ensure that its area is inspected from time to time to detect statutory nuisances, and, where a complaint is brought, it must take such steps as are reasonably practicable to investigate the complaint. Schedule 3 of the Act gives the local authority powers to enter premises for this purpose. Where a local authority is satisfied about the existence of a statutory nuisance, it must serve an abatement notice on the person responsible, in other words on the person by whose act, default or sufferance the nuisance arises or continues (section 79(7)). Where the person responsible cannot be found, then the local authority must serve the notice on the owner or the occupier of the premises. However, if the nuisance arises as a result of a structural defect the notice must be served on the owner.

The notice must require the person on whom it is served to abate the nuisance and to take such steps or carry out such works as are required to abate the nuisance. Where the local authority requires specific works to be carried out, the notice should give sufficient particulars to enable the receipient of the notice to know exactly what is required. The abatement notice must also contain specific time limits within which the receipient of the notice must carry out the works.

Action by tenants

Although the primary duty under the 1990 Act for enforcement lies on local authorities, and they may exercise these powers against housing associations, the main use to which the powers have been put in disrepair cases is for individuals to take action against local authority landlords, since a local authority cannot serve an abatement notice on itself.

Person aggrieved

A person may be "aggrieved" by a nuisance not only if he or she is a tenant, but also if a licensee or other occupier, such as a family member or lodger (section 82(1)). Each person must, however, be able to show that he or she is individually affected by the matters being complained of, and a "joint" action by all tenants affected by a particular problem will not be appropriate.

Case report

Birmingham City Council, which owned a large block of flats, was subject to proceedings brought by a number of tenants alleging that the block was a statutory nuisance. The tenants complained about defects both in the common parts and in the flats. In the magistrates' court the tenants produced evidence of nuisance only in relation to 16 of the flats, but the magistrate found that the problems in those flats – of condensation and mould growth – were symptomatic of the block as a whole, and ordered the local authority to carry out works to the whole of the block. On appeal, the court held that since each complainant has to be a person aggrieved in relation to the statutory nuisance, there has to be a personal link between the cause of the statutory nuisance and the person complaining. This link could only be established for each complainant in relation to his or her own flat. Therefore to be successful all the tenants should have brought their own actions. *Birmingham District Council v McMahon* (1987) 19 HLR 452

Person responsible

Proceedings have to be brought against the person responsible for the nuisance or, where the defects are structural or the person responsible cannot be found, against the owner (section 82(4)). A person is responsible for a nuisance if he or she is the person, to "whose act, default or sufferance the nuisance is attributable" (section 79(7) of the 1990 Act).

This may mean that the social landlord can argue that the tenant is responsible for the nuisance.

> *Case report*
> Ms Warner was the tenant of the London Borough of
> Lambeth. The premises had been rehabilitated short-
> ly before she moved in. In October 1980 an outbreak
> of dry rot was found in one of the rooms. The tenant
> found she could not tolerate the works while she was
> in occupation and therefore refused access to the
> workers. In 1981 the authority tried again to do the
> works but the tenant wanted to be rehoused. From
> May 1982 the local authority made three offers of
> alternative accommodation all of which were
> refused. In December 1982 the tenant took proceed-
> ings against local authority for statutory nuisance.
> The defects were held to constitute a statutory
> nuisance but no order was made by the magistrates
> since the tenant was deemed to be the person
> by whose act, default or sufferance the nuisance
> continued. The finding was upheld on appeal.
> *Warner v London Borough of Lambeth* (1984) 15 HLR 42

One of the most frequent problems where statutory
nuisance proceedings are used is that of condensation
dampness. Some social landlords have successfully
defended prosecutions under the 1990 Act (and its predecessor) on the basis that the tenants alone were
responsible for the dampness.

> *Case report*
> Action was taken against Dover District Council by
> six tenants alleging that their homes were a statutory
> nuisance due to condensation problems. The council
> argued that the condensation was due to the failure
> of the tenants to use the electric central heating system.
> The tenants failed to use the system because of its
> expense, and instead used cheaper paraffin or calor

gas heaters, which produced much greater water vapour. The Court of Appeal found that had the central heating been used properly the houses would not have been prejudicial to health. The statutory nuisance accordingly arose because of the act or default of the tenants, even though their refusal to use the system on account of expense was wholly understandable. *Dover District Council v Farrar* (1980) 2 HLR 32

A landlord must, however, provide adequate ventilation, insulation and heating.

Case report
The Greater London Council were owners of a flat which was situated on the corner of a block. The flat was on the ground floor, but was so constructed that this level was raised from the ground, so that not only were three sides of the flat exposed to the elements, but so was the whole of the underneath. As originally constructed the flat had a solid fuel fire in the living room. Subsequently the flues were found to be defective, so that they were blocked and the fire place removed and replaced with an electric heater. One storage heater was provided. The tenant used three oil fires and an electric fire, keeping the heating on all or for a major part of the day. The flat nonetheless suffered from severe condensation dampness. The GLC was prosecuted by the London Borough of Tower Hamlets, and found responsible for the statutory nuisance.

On appeal the GLC sought to argue that the tenant was responsible for the nuisance. This argument was rejected; the cause of the dampness was the failure of the landlord to take necessary precautions, either by way of ventilation or insulation, or by providing any special form of heating, for a property which was wholly exceptionally vulnerable to condensation. An adequate combination of ventilation, insulation and heating must be provided in order to make the premises habitable. However, where sufficient heating or ventilation was provided the onus shifted to the tenant who was obliged to make use of the facilities. So long as the landlord has done everything reasonably practicable and the cause of the continuing condensation is that the tenant chooses not to use the facilities supplied (because of the cost or otherwise) then the landlord is not the person responsible for the nuisance. *GLC v London Borough of Tower Hamlets* (1983) 15 HLR 54

Very high heating costs may be the result of inadequate insulation. If the landlord has not provided a building in which there is adequate insulation – there is now a standard measurement under the National Home Energy Rating (see P. Reddin *Dealing with Disrepair*, ch. 8 p. 135) – whether the tenant uses the heating or not, it is still arguable the landlord has not fulfilled the requirement to provide an adequate combination of ventilation, insulation and heating. The landlord should not be able to shift the whole onus on the tenant simply by claiming that there is a central heating system, when it is the inadequacy of the building which makes the heating prohibitively expensive to run.

Where the landlord is not in breach of any repairing obligations, it may still be the organisation by whose act or sufferance the nuisance continues. For example where dampness is due to a design defect which causes no dis-repair within the meaning of section 11 of the Landlord and Tenant Act 1985 (see above p. 30), there may remain liability under the 1990 Act where the heating, ventilation or insulation is inadequate (*Birmingham District Council v Kelly* (1987) 19 HLR 452).

Procedure

Under section 82 the complainant is not required to serve an abatement notice. Instead, the complainant will begin the proceedings by laying an information before a magistrate. However, by section 82(5) a complainant is required to give notice in writing of intention to bring proceedings and to specify the matter complained of. Except in the case of a nuisance falling within section 79(1)(g) (noise pollution), the period of notice required is 21 days. Where such a notice is served – and the landlord considers that there is no defence to the action – steps should be taken to ensure that the nuisance is brought to an end in order to avoid potential liabilities to fines and costs.

The magistrates' court has a variety of options when dealing with a statutory nuisance. If satisfied of the existence of a statutory nuisance, it must make a nuisance order requiring abatement of the nuisance. It may also order the execution of works to prevent its recurrence and/or impose a fine. Where the court is satisfied that the nuisance exists and renders the premises unfit for human habitation, the court may prohibit use of the premises until rendered fit (section 82(3)).

If the order is not complied with for no "reasonable excuse" further proceedings may be taken and the defaulter may be fined and repeatedly fined (section

82(8)). It is for the magistrate to decide whether a statutory nuisance existed, whether it has been abated and, if not abated, the steps that are necessary to abate the nuisance.

Because of the wording of the Act, the relevant date on which the magistrates are to consider whether a nuisance exists – or if abated, is likely to recur – is the date of the hearing of the information, rather than the date of laying the information. Since the court is obliged to make an abatement order if the nuisance is found to exist (there is no discretion), it is the issue of whether the nuisance exists at the date of the hearing which is vital.

The purpose of the legislation is to provide an effective means of requiring landlords to abate nuisances (see e.g. *London Borough of Hackney v Carr* (1994) *The Times* 9 March). This is so even if the works are carried out after the beginning of the case, for example, where the case goes part-heard. The magistrates' power to award compensation flows from the entering of a conviction, which will not happen until all the evidence is heard and the case concluded.

Compensation orders

Compensation may also be awarded by a magistrates' court for damage resulting from a statutory nuisance. This is not, however, under the 1990 Act but under the court's more general powers to award compensation for any personal injury, loss or damage resulting from an offence for which a defendant has been convicted: section 35 Powers of Criminal Courts Act 1973 (as amended). Nevertheless the power to make compensation orders still exists in proceedings under the 1990 Act (*Botross v London Borough of Hammersmith & Fulham*

(1994) 27 HLR 179). Compensation can be ordered in addition to any other penalty (*Herbert v London Borough of Lambeth* (1991) 24 HLR 299).

Levels of compensation
The maximum award is £5,000 for each offence (Magistrates' Courts Act 1980, as amended). The award may be made "on application or otherwise", i.e. such orders may be made on the initiative of the magistrates themselves as well as on the application of a person affected by the existence of the statutory nuisance. The principles for calculating the sums on which such compensation orders are based are not set out in detail in the legislation but have been added to and expanded by case law.

• The loss must be actually suffered (*R v Vivian* [1979] 1 All ER 48)

• It is not necessary to show that the landlord would have been liable in civil proceedings (*R v Chappell* [1984] Crim LR 574)

• If a claim is made for personal injury, full details should be provided (*R v Cooper* [1982] Crim LR 308)

• Injury may include fear and anxiety (*Bond v Chief Constable of Kent* [1983] 1 All ER 456).

Causation
An underlying principle in assessing compensation awards is that the loss or damage must result from the offence. Thus the order cannot deal with matters which were not the subject of the proceedings in the magistrates court. In this context it is only loss or damage which is attributable to the statutory nuisance which may be compensated, not broader matters

which might arise in cases of disrepair or other types of civil proceeding. In *Herbert v London Borough of Lambeth* (above) it was held not to be an appropriate use of the powers under section 35 of the Magistrates Courts Act for a magistrates' court to award compensation for damages which could loosely be described as personal injury. If compensation for that sort of injury is to be awarded, it is preferable that it should be dealt with in the course of civil proceedings in the county court.

In determining whether loss or damage resulted from the offence the usual, strict rules about causation are not to be adopted. Instead the court must ask itself whether the loss or damage can fairly be said to have resulted from the relevant offence (*R v Thomson Holidays* [1973] QB 592).

Appeals

A defendant who has been ordered to pay compensation may appeal to the Court of Appeal, which has wide powers to vary or annul the compensation order. (A compensation order can be reviewed by the court which made it even after the time for appealing has passed.) A defendant can also appeal against conviction or sentence to the Crown Court, and this takes the form of a rehearing. The court remains confined, however, to considering the matters as they were at the date of the magistrates' court hearing.

Costs

Legal aid is not available to tenants to fund bringing Criminal proceedings under section 82 of the 1990 Act. Costs may, however, be awarded if the action is successful. Where the court is satisfied that the alleged statutory nuisance existed at the date the information was laid then, irrespective of whether the nuisance has since been abated or is unlikely to recur, the court is obliged under section 82(12) of the Act to order the defendant to pay "such amount as the court considers reasonably sufficient to compensate [the complainant] for any expenses properly incurred by them in the proceedings."

Where, however, solicitors agree to act for tenants on the basis that they will only be charged if costs are awarded, there may have been no costs properly incurred.

Case report

Mrs Norman successfully prosecuted the British Waterways Board, her landlord, for a statutory nuisance at her home. The magistrates ordered that the Board pay her costs. Mrs Norman was on income support, and the solicitors had not discussed with her the charges they would make if the case was lost. It was clearly the expectation of both the solicitors and Mrs Norman that they would only be paid if the case was won. On appeal against the order for costs, the Court of Appeal held that Mrs Norman had not incurred any costs for which an order could be made under section 82(12). Furthermore the agreement was a contingency and accordingly contrary to public policy. *British Waterways Board v Norman* (1993) 26 HLR 232

Contingency fees

It is possible for tenants to make an arrangement with solicitors which is effective. In the *Norman* case the court stated that it would have been lawful to have an agreement that the payment of the solicitors costs could be deferred until the outcome of the case was known. At that stage, provided that it had not formed the basis of the agreement with the client, it would be open to the solicitors to decide not to enforce their right to be paid.

Other public health provisions

In addition to and separate from the powers and duties contained in the Environmental Protection Act 1990, there remain in the Public Health Acts and Building Acts, ancillary duties placed on local authorities. While these duties are not necessarily enforceable between the parties the provisions are important to local authorities charged with managing the housing stock. Some of the more common examples of these are set out below.

Sanitary facilities
By virtue of section 64 of the Building Act 1984 (as amended) local authorities have a duty to serve notice on an owner of premises requiring the provision of WCs if a building (or any part of a building occupied as a separate dwelling) has insufficient toilet facilities, or such facilities which are present are in such a state as to be prejudicial to health or a nuisance (and cannot be made satisfactory without reconstruction). The person served with such a notice has a right of appeal by which he or she can challenge the notice. If the person is unsuccessful on appeal (or does not appeal at all) the local authority may carry out the works in default and

recoup the cost from the person served.

The Public Health Act 1936 also provides for a number of offences related to the provision of sanitary facilities.

Drains and sewers

Sections 21 and 59 of the Building Act 1984 gives local authorities powers to require owners to make satisfactory provision for drainage and sewage. These powers enable a local authority to require not only the owner but also the occupier to take remedial action, for example where there is a blockage.

Vermin

Under section 83 of the Public Health Act 1936 a local authority must take action where premises are filthy or in such a condition as to be prejudicial to health or verminous. If that is the case the local authority should serve a notice on the owner or occupier requiring such steps to be taken for removing or destroying the vermin. In the case of non-compliance by the owner or occupier the local authority may carry out works in default and seek recompense from the person served. In some circumstances, such as cockroach infestation in a block of flats, the local authority itself may be liable in nuisance (see further at p. 49).

Fire precautions and dilapidation

The local authority has further powers, contained in the Building Act 1984, in relation to dangerous or dilapidated buildings, or where fire precautions are inadequate.

CHAPTER 7

TENANT'S CONTRACTUAL OBLIGATIONS

Tenant-like user / Acts of waste /
Landlord's remedy **/ Landlord's remedies for
breach /** *Possession of the premises /
Damages / Injunctions*

Social landlords and housing managers having read this far would be forgiven for thinking that only the landlord has any responsibility for the maintenance and repair of the property. Indeed, the complaint is often voiced in court that there is only so much managers can do if tenants fail to look after the property on a day-to-day basis or if the tenant fails to tell the landlord about a defect early enough to avoid consequential damage. The failure to notify the landlord has been dealt with elsewhere in this book where it will be seen that it *could* result in no liability at all being found, or, a reduction in damages due to the tenant's failure to mitigate his or her loss. But what if the tenant actually causes or exacerbates a defect?

Many social rented sector agreements contain an express term requiring the tenant to carry out certain items of repair and/or decoration. If, however, the agreement is silent or vague on the issue there will be implied into the agreement an obligation on the tenant to use the premises in a "tenant-like manner"; and an obligation not to commit acts of waste.

Tenant-like user

A tenant is under an implied obligation at common law to use the premises he or she is given in a "tenant-like manner". However, this duty is limited in scope. It is not an obligation to repair but, rather, to use the premises in a proper manner and to refrain from acts which would amount to a breach of the duty.

The scope of the obligation has been described as "the little jobs about the place which a reasonable tenant would do" (*Warren v Keen* [1954] 1 QB 15). So, for example, a tenant should unblock sinks, mend electric lights and so on. Beyond this the tenant will not be liable for disrepair. What amounts to "tenant-like" user will depend on all the circumstances and what is deemed to be reasonable in those circumstances.

Examples of when a tenant could be found to be in breach of the obligation include:

• introduction of vermin or cockroaches into the premises

• leaving premises in the middle of winter for a prolonged period of time without heating or draining of the system so that the pipes burst

• blocking of sinks or WCs

• failing to take any steps to remedy a simple leak.

Acts of waste

This is often cited as a separate duty imposed on tenants. However it could more properly be described as part of the obligation of a "tenant-like user". In other words tenant-like use requires a tenant to repair acts of waste committed by him or her.

Waste is damage to, destruction of, or alteration of any part of the premises let to the tenant which will reduce the value of the premises to the person entitled to have the premises back at the end of the letting. It must be remembered that the *de minimis* rule (i.e. there can be no claim where the reduction in value of the property is minimal) will apply to cases of alleged waste. This will be particularly relevant where a social landlord is seeking to balance the costs of pursuing a tenant for damages against the likely reward. If a tenant has carried out an alteration which actually enhances the value of the premises (although not where the nature of the premises has been changed) or has only a minimal negative effect the remedy will normally not be available, or if available a damages award will be very low.

Where damage is caused to premises in the course of reasonable and proper use this will not amount to waste. However, where acts of the tenant have caused damage the onus will be on the tenant to show that the way in which the premises were being used was reasonable. Further, any acts which are sanctioned by the landlord will not amount to waste.

Actions which will amount to waste include:
- alteration of the internal structure
- removal of fixtures and fittings

- damage to doors/windows.

Liability for waste extends to licensees – in fact to any occupier who is not a trespasser.

Landlord's remedy

Where acts of waste have been committed the landlord may seek damages or an injunction (to prevent the continued behaviour and/or to put the premises back into a proper condition) or both. In order to satisfy the court that such remedy should be awarded it will be essential that the landlord supplies full particulars of the nature and extent of the waste. This information is best presented in the form of a qualified surveyor's report.

Landlord's remedies for breach

Breach of the implied terms will sometimes necessitate the landlord taking action. In other cases, where the letting is on a lease of greater than seven years the tenant may be under express repairing covenants. For shorter leases there may be express covenants as to the repair and decoration of the internal parts of the dwelling.

The remedies available to a landlord for breach of such obligations are different to those available to a tenant, though similarly based on either an express or implied covenant. Even where damages and specific performance (remedies available to both tenants and landlords) are claimed, the considerations relevant to their award will be different.

Once the landlord suspects that the tenant is in breach of covenant, a decision must be taken about which remedy to pursue. The choice will depend on the desired result of enforcing the covenant. It is important from the outset that the housing manager clearly identifies the intended objective and that the chosen remedy is appropriate to that.

Possession of the premises

Tenants have a certain amount of protection against eviction and proceedings can only be brought for possession on the basis of breach of covenant contained in the tenancy agreement, where one of the grounds provided in the relevant legislation is made out. Which particular piece of legislation to apply depends on the identity of the landlord and the date of commencement of the agreement.

Landlord	Date of Tenancy	Relevant Act
Local Authority	Any time	Housing Act 1985
Housing Association	Prior to 15.1.89	Housing Act 1985
Housing Association	On or after 15.1.89	Housing Act 1988

See generally A. Dymond *Security of Tenure* Arden's Housing Library vol. 1, 1995; and A. Dymond *Presenting Possession Proceedings* Arden's Housing Library vol. 4, 1996.

Grounds for possession

Schedule 2 to the Housing Act 1985 contains two grounds on which a landlord can seek to recover possession from the tenant on the basis of the tenant's use of the premises. Ground 1 provides that the landlord may recover possession where "... an obligation of the tenancy has been broken or not performed"; and Ground 3, that "the condition of the dwelling-house or any of the common parts has deteriorated owing to acts of waste by, or the neglect or default of, the tenant or a person residing in the dwelling-house and, in the case of an act of waste by, or the neglect or default of, a person lodging with the tenant or a sub-tenant of his, the tenant has not taken such steps as he ought reasonably to have taken for the removal of the lodger or sub-tenant."

Schedule 2 to the Housing Act 1988 also contains two grounds on which a landlord can seek to recover possession from the tenant on the basis of the tenant's use of the premises. These are: Ground 12 covering any obligation of the tenancy (other than one related to the payment of rent) which has been broken or not performed; and Ground 13, which is in the same terms as Ground 3 of the 1985 Act.

All the grounds are discretionary and the court will only order possession where it is considered reasonable so to do. See further A. Dymond *Security of Tenure*, ch. 9, Arden's Housing Library vol. 1, 1995.

Damages

In theory damages will be recoverable against a tenant who is in breach of covenant (either express or implied) contained in the tenancy agreement. Whether this is an appropriate remedy in practice will depend on the facts of each case and in particular on the financial means of the tenant. Where a tenant is without means there will be no point in pursuing him or her for damages.

In an action for damages based on the destruction of the premises, compensation will be awarded to reflect the reduction in value of the premises. For this reason it is helpful to include in any report the likely fall in value directly attributable to the tenant's behaviour. Where a tenant is in breach of the obligation to use the premises in a tenant-like manner and that breach has resulted in damage or deterioration which has not been rectified, the landlord can alternatively pursue the tenant for the cost of the works.

If the landlord has reserved an express right to enter the premises to remedy disrepair which is the tenant's responsibility and then recover the cost of doing so, then this will be an adequate remedy in itself. If, however, the tenancy agreement is silent on this aspect, then a right of entry will be implied into the agreement by virtue of the corresponding obligation implied on the landlord to carry out works if premises are in a state of disrepair.

Injunctions
The priority in some cases will be to carry out works urgently to prevent further deterioration or disaster and only emergency legal proceedings will be appropriate.

Where an injunction is sought it must be shown that the acts of waste committed by the tenant are such as will cause or threaten substantial damage to the value of the premises for the person to whom they will revert at the end of the period of the letting. If the acts are continuing and have caused actual damage, the landlord can claim damages for the loss of value and, at the same time, an injunction to restrain the continuance of the acts of destruction or alteration.

CHAPTER 8

GETTING THE WORKS DONE

Right to enter to repair / *Enforcement through injunction* / *Access to neighbouring land* / **Requiring tenant to move** / *Grounds for possession* / *Tenant's security of tenure* / **Payments to tenants**

Having accepted that work of repair or improvement is required to a social landlord's property and having approached the tenant for his or her co-operation, housing managers sometimes find that tenants are not as keen as they may expect and, rather than going to court to force the landlord to take action, some tenants are actually loathe to let the landlord or its workers onto the premises.

Similarly, where the landlord wishes to inspect the property it may have difficulty gaining access for this purpose. The tenant may be resisting this action for perfectly proper reasons, such as young children with asthma being affected by dust, or elderly people who may be afraid to let strangers into their property.

Each occasion requires the housing manager to be sensitive to the real reason why the tenant is not co-operating. However, at the end of the day there may be a real need or indeed obligation to enter the property and in those circumstances the landlord can use court proceedings to force the tenant to permit access to it and its contractors.

Sometimes it may be necessary to move the tenants out of the property for the duration of the works. It may be the case that it is necessary or even obligatory to make payments to the tenants to secure their co-operation.

Right to enter to repair

The right to enter must be either expressly reserved or implied into the tenancy. In some situations the landlord will have an implied right to enter the premises to carry out repairs. Whenever a landlord has expressly covenanted to keep the premises in repair it will have the right to enter the premises to inspect and carry out any necessary works. This is also the case where the landlord is under a statutory obligation to keep the premises in repair as in section 11 of the Landlord and Tenant Act 1985: section 11(6).

Where the landlord has this right (whether by express term, implied licence or statutory licence) then it may be exercised by entering the premises and carrying out all necessary works of repair. If those works are within the tenant's covenant the landlord may then, additionally, recover the cost of the works from the tenant.

The right of entry must be exercised reasonably and this requires that the landlord notifies the tenant about the nature and extent of the proposed works, but not necessarily a full specification of works. If the landlord gives sufficient notice and the tenant nevertheless refuses access then it is strongly arguable that the land-lord is not in breach of its repairing obligation for so long as the tenant continues to refuse. If the tenant then brings an action for damages for disrepair the refusal of access should be pleaded as a defence to the claim.

Enforcement through injunction

Where a tenant is continuing to refuse access to the landlord's surveyor or workers it may be necessary to enforce the right to enter by seeking an injunction requiring the tenant to permit access. The landlord should first notify the tenant in writing of the intention to seek an injunction. If the tenant still refuses access an application should be made to the county court for an injunction. (For a precedent see Appendix III).

Access to neighbouring land

Occasionally, a landlord will need to get onto land adjoining the property which requires repair, in order to effect those repairs. When the landlord has no con-tractual or common law right to enter onto that land because it is in private ownership, for example, it may rely on the Access to Neighbouring Land Act 1992.

An application may be made to the county court in the first instance for an "access order". It is the owner or occupier of the property in need of repair (or their contractors) who can make the application.

The basis of the application is that the works are

necessary for the preservation of the property and they cannot be carried out, or would be substantially more difficult to carry out, without the required access.

Requiring tenant to move

While the case law is not entirely clear, it seems to be accepted that the tenant may be obliged to move where it is strictly essential for the premises to be vacant to enable completion of the works. In other words the landlord has an implied licence to occupy the premises for a reasonable time in order to do that which it has covenanted to do and has a right to do. For this purpose the covenant that the tenant should enjoy quiet enjoyment of the premises (see chapter 3, p. 46 above) is qualified.

The Court of Appeal explained the principles to be applied to this problem: "this right to enter and occupy must be limited to that which is strictly necessary in order to do the work of repair. The obligation to allow the landlord to enter and occupy in order to effect repairs does not seem to us to involve a further obligation to give the landlord exclusive occupation ... nor does it involve an obligation to give him access to all parts of the house at the same time unless again this is essential." (*McGreal v Wake* (1984) 13 HLR 134).

Thus, where major works of repair are being considered the landlord must decide whether these works can be done with the tenant in residence or not. If they cannot, and negotiations with the tenant prove fruitless, then strictly speaking the landlord is entitled simply to obtain access and commence the works, since there will be no breach by the landlord of its obligations. In order to avoid confrontation and to ensure there is no illegality in any procedure used, landlords should not just seek to start works without the tenant's agreement.

Grounds for possession

If possession is required then it can be sought under one of the relevant Grounds of the Housing Act 1985 or 1988. (See further A. Dymond *Security of Tenure* Arden's Housing Library vol. 1, 1995). Ground 10 of the 1985 Act sets out a mandatory ground for possession of a secure tenancy where, provided suitable alternative accommodation is provided, the landlord intends within a reasonable time of seeking possession to do one of the following:

• demolish or reconstruct the building, or part of the building which includes the dwelling-house

• carry out work on the building, or on land let together with the building.

In either case, the landlord must also be able to demonstrate that the works cannot reasonably be done without obtaining possession. This is a matter on which expert evidence should be obtained.

For assured tenants, Ground 6 of the Housing Act 1988 enables the landlord to obtain vacant possession to carry out works to the premises. The landlord must intend to demolish or reconstruct the whole or a substantial part of the premises, or carry out substantial works on them. It is a condition of the applicability of the Ground that the intended work cannot reasonably be carried out without the tenant giving up possession of the dwelling-house for the following reasons:

1. the tenant is unwilling to agree to such a variation of the terms of the tenancy as would give such access and other facilities as would permit the intended work to be carried out;

2. the nature of the intended work is such that no such variation is practicable;

3. the tenant is not willing to accept an assured tenancy of such part only of the dwelling-house as would leave in the possession of the landlord so much of the dwelling-house as would be reasonable to enable the intended work to be carried out and, where appropriate, as would give such access and other facilities over the reduced part as would permit the intended work to be carried out;

4. the nature of the intended work is such that such a tenancy is not practicable.

The Ground is also available to a registered housing association, or a charitable housing trust, where the person intending to do the works is not the landlord, but a superior landlord. The Ground is not available to a landlord who has brought the property for money, or money's worth, with the tenant in occupation. Again expert evidence about the applicability of the Ground will be important. While the Ground is mandatory and does not bring with it the right to suitable alternative accommodation, many housing associations will want to offer suitable alternative accommodation in these circumstances.

Tenant's security of tenure

If the tenant is being moved for works to be carried out, some thought needs to be given to the tenant's status while in the alternative accommodation.

Permanent moves
Where the move is permanent, no problems should arise. Council tenants will become secure tenants of the new accommodation. For tenants of housing associations, if the tenancy they are leaving was assured, the new tenancy will also be assured. For those leaving secure tenancies, the new tenancy may still be secure, notwithstanding that it commences after the Housing Act 1988 came into force (section 35(4)(d) Housing Act 1988).

Temporary moves
If the new letting is intended to be temporary, the situation is more problematic. If, as is likely, all the conditions for the grant of a secure or, as the case may be, assured tenancy are satisfied in the temporary home (see A. Dymond *Security of Tenure,* chs. 3 and 4, Arden's Housing Library vol. 1) there is no relevant exemption to prevent security attaching to the temporary home. One argument which may be made is that the "only or principal home" of the tenant remains that where the works are being carried out, and therefore no security attaches to the temporary home. This argument is more likely to succeed where the move is intended to be very short.

Ground 8 of the Housing Act 1985 makes provision for possession to be obtained from a secure tenant following the completion of works to the tenant's original home. The landlord must be able to establish that:
1. the dwelling-house was made available for occupation by the tenant (or a predecessor) while works were carried out on the dwelling-house which he or she previously occupied as his or her only or principal home;
2. the tenant (or a predecessor) was a secure tenant of

the other dwelling-house at the time when he or she ceased to occupy it as his or her home;

3. the tenant (or a predecessor) accepted the tenancy of the dwelling-house of which possession is sought on the understanding that he or she would give up occupation when, on completion of the works, the other dwelling-house was again available for occupation by him or her under a secure tenancy;

4. the works have been completed and the other dwelling-house is so available.

The Ground for possession is discretionary, so that the landlord will have to show that it is reasonable to grant possession. Various factors will be relevant to the question of reasonableness: the reasons for the works being undertaken; how long the tenant was in occupation of the former home; how long the works took to be completed and consequently how long the tenant has been in the second home; how long the tenant was told the works would take.

For assured tenants there is no equivalent ground available. Housing associations could, however, simply use Ground 9 of the Housing Act 1988, i.e. suitable alternative accommodation. The accommodation being offered could be the original home. Since Ground 9 is discretionary the issues about how long the tenants have been in the "temporary" accommodation will be relevant to obtaining possession.

Payments to tenants

Where possession is obtained under Ground 10 of the Housing Act 1985, or where a registered housing association obtains possession in order to carry out an improvement or redevelopment the tenant has the right to home loss payments under the Land Compensation Act 1973.

Where there is no "right" to payments or where the displacement is not permanent, social landlords may want to consider voluntary payments to secure the co-operation of tenants. The level of such payments is for the landlord to decide.

Where the works are not being carried out following a breach of the repairing covenant by the landlord – for example because the works are ones of improvement or are being carried out within a reasonable period of being notified of the disrepair – then the tenant has no "right" to monetary payment. It is only where there has been a breach and the sums are awardable as damages (see above chapter 5) that a tenant can force payment from the landlord.

Case report
Mr and Mrs McDougall were tenants of Easington District Council. They lived in a system-built house made of pre-fabricated concrete, which had a number of design defects. In December 1985 the McDougalls moved out in order that extensive works could be carried out to the house. On moving back in, five months later, they discovered that redecoration was needed to restore the house to its previous internal condition. *McDougall v Easington DC* (1989) 22 HLR 310

The tenants claimed that the works were works of repair under the repairing covenant implied by section 11 of the Landlord and Tenant Act 1985 and that therefore they were entitled to damages, including the cost of redecoration (see above, p. 28). The Court of Appeal decided the works were improvement and not repair (see above p. 30). Accordingly the tenants were only entitled to the £50 which had been promised to them before they moved out.

CHAPTER 9

IMPROVEMENTS

*Improvements by tenant / Statutory right
to improve / Compensation for improvements /
Rent following an improvement /
Improvements by landlord*

In addition to repairing the property the landlord –
particularly a social landlord – or tenant may wish
to improve or alter it. This chapter looks first at the
rights of tenants to improve, and secondly, at those
of landlords.

Improvements by tenant

At common law there is no limitation on the tenant's
right to improve the property except where the
improvement is an act of waste (see chapter 7, above) or
the alterations would be in breach of an express repairing covenant. It is therefore common for tenancy agreements to have a clause which limits the right to improve,
sometimes altogether and sometimes permitting
improvements but subject to the landlord's consent. For
secure tenants special provision is made in the Housing

Act 1985. Improvement for this purpose includes:
- any addition to or alteration in the landlord's fixtures and fittings
- any addition or alteration connected with the provision of services to the dwelling
- the erection of a radio or television aerial (and also probably a satellite dish)
- the carrying out of external decoration.

Statutory right to improve

Sections 97 to 101 of the Housing Act 1985, govern the operation of the right. By section 97 there is a right to improve but only with the landlord's consent. The consent cannot be withheld unreasonably and if it is it will be implied that consent was given. Where the tenant goes ahead with the improvements even though the landlord has refused consent, an injunction could be sought by the landlord preventing the works continuing, or requiring e.g. that an aerial is removed, on the basis that the works are a breach of the tenancy agreement. At the hearing of the application it would be for the landlord to show that the consent has been reasonably refused.

By section 99 of the Housing Act a local authority may give its consent to improvements subject to conditions, but the conditions must also be reasonable. If consent is given subject to an unreasonable condition then it will be deemed that consent was unreasonably withheld (and therefore consent will be implied without the condition). Where there is a dispute about whether a condition was reasonable or unreasonable the burden is on the local authority to show it was reasonable. Where a tenant has not complied with a reasonable condition then this will be treated as a breach of an obligation of the tenancy agreement.

There are no equivalent provisions in the Housing Act 1988. For housing associations it will be necessary to include an express provision in the tenancy agreement, which seeks to achieve the same; see for example the Model Assured Tenancy produced by the National Federation of Housing Associations.

Compensation for improvements

New rights to compensation for improvements were created by section 122 of the Leasehold Reform, Housing and Urban Development Act 1993 (which inserted new sections 99A and 99B into the Housing Act 1985 with effect from 1 February 1994). The conditions which must be satisfied are that:

- a secure tenant has made an improvement and the work on the improvement was begun not earlier than 1 February 1994
- the local authority has given its consent (whether express or deemed to have been given) and
- at the time when the tenancy comes to an end the landlord is a local authority and the tenancy is a secure tenancy.

The Secure Tenants of Local Authorities (Compensation for Improvements) Regulations 1994 became operative on 1 April 1994 and limit the type of improvements which may be compensated and the amount of compensation.

Discretionary payments

A local authority may make a discretionary payment if an improvement does not fall within the mandatory compensation scheme. Where a secure tenant has made an improvement and the work was begun on or after 3 October 1980 – and the improvement has materially added to the price for which the premises may be sold on the open market, or added to the rent which the landlord may be expected to charge on letting the premises – then the landlord may make (at or after the end of the tenancy) such payment to the tenant as the landlord considers to be appropriate (section 100).

Rent following an improvement

Where a secure tenant has carried out a lawful improvement for which he or she has not recovered the cost, the rent must not be increased to reflect the value of the improved premises (section 101 of the Housing Act 1985). Where the tenant has recovered some or all of the cost of the improvement then an increased rent may be considered but taking into account only that part of the improvement for which the tenant has recovered the cost.

Improvements by landlord

A landlord may wish to make an improvement to premises but can usually only do so where the tenant consents. If the tenant does not consent to the improvement (and, unlike landlords, there would not appear to be any implied term that the tenant must be reasonable) then whether or not the landlord can enter and carry out works will depend on the security the tenant enjoys:

• if the occupier is a periodic secure tenant/licensee or

an assured tenant then the landlord will have to obtain a court order under one of the grounds for possession (see chapter 8)

• if the occupier is a fixed-term secure tenant/licensee (very rare) or a fixed-term assured tenant then, unless the agreement specifically provides for the landlord to carry out improvements, the landlord can do nothing until the end of the fixed term and then will have to get a court order

• if the occupier is a periodic non-secure occupier then the landlord can simply terminate the agreement and regain possession

• if the occupier is a fixed term non-secure occupier then nothing can be done until the end of the fixed term (in the absence of express provision).

Some tenancy agreements include a clause requiring the tenant to give access for works of improvement. It is advisable to include such a term to avoid the tenant being able to refuse access. In such a case, if the tenant does refuse access then an injunction may be sought to require compliance with the term, or possession may be sought for breach of the tenancy agreement.

CHAPTER 10

COURT PROCEEDINGS

**Which court? / Evidence / Court etiquette /
Procedure / Housing managers' evidence /
Experts' evidence / Statutory nuisance in
the magistrates' court / Judgments and
orders / Conclusion**

Some disputes will eventually end up in court and the
parties will suffer the expense of proceeding to a fully
contested trial. The English legal system remains an
adversarial one which can at times seem opaque. This
chapter outlines the procedure which will be followed
at trial and guidance for those attending about what
may, or may not, happen on the day.

Which court?

The majority of cases with which housing managers
and officers are concerned will be dealt with in the
civil jurisdiction of the county court. The current upper
level of damages which may be awarded in the county
court is £50,000. The claim must be estimated to be
worth more than £5,000 if it is to be heard in the

county court as of right. This figure must be included in the pleadings, as absence of any reference to the level of damages claimed will automatically result in the claim being processed as a claim for damages of less than £5,000. If the damages claimed are in excess of £50,000 the case will be automatically referred to the High Court.

Claims estimated to be worth between £3,000 and £5,000 may be referred to the small claims court. The new small claims court upper limit is £3,000. There is no reason why disrepair claims, even those involving claims for specific performance, will not be dealt with at the small claims court. However, plaintiffs may argue that although the damages claimed are less than £3,000, the value of the works to be carried out in respect of a claim for specific performance brings the "amount involved" to more than the small claims limit (CCR Order 19 rule 3(1)). Legal aid is not provided for small claims dispute resolution, and costs orders (such as are seen in the county court) are not appropriate.

Evidence

Whether the evidence is to be given orally or in written form will depend on whether the matter is heard in open court or in chambers. It is usual practice for inter-locutory matters, e.g. applications for injunctions, to be heard in chambers. Some courts will also occasionally hear rent arrears claims, and any disrepair counter-claim, in chambers. If the matter is being heard in chambers, the parties are entitled, subject to the judge ordering oral evidence or any party requesting that the witness attends for cross-examination, to give their evidence by way of sworn affidavit (CCR Order 20 rule 5). Some applications before a full trial must be supported by affidavit, e.g. an application for an interlocutory repairing injunction.

It is extremely important that the affidavit is prepared carefully and accurately. Housing officers may be asked to prepare affidavits either to support an application (e.g. for an injuction requiring access) or to resist an application. (e.g. for works to be done). In either case the affidavit must set out the facts relied on and the reasons why the judge should be persuaded to grant or refuse the application. The person who is to swear the affidavit must be absolutely clear about what is being stated and must be able to attest to the truth of the contents. An affidavit should be prepared in the light of the legal framework for the application and should set out the facts required to sustain the argument. Any documents which are to be tendered as proof must be attached to the affidavit and be sworn to be true copies.

Evidence in open court should be given orally. The witness will be examined in chief (i.e. questioned by his or her own lawyer) and then cross-examined by the lawyer representing the other party. The witness should have prepared a witness statement in advance which will have been served on the other side, and should be familiar with its contents. See further P. Reddin *Dealing with Disrepair*, ch. 9 p. 142.

Cross-examination can appear daunting to many people. However, if the evidence is given in a clear and honest way there is little can go wrong – in theory. Legal representatives are there not to reduce a witness to tears but to assist the court in coming to a just conclusion!

It is only what the witness actually knows that can be referred to in evidence. Second-hand information is hearsay and cannot be cited by anyone other than the party with direct knowledge of it, subject to the exceptions to the rule against hearsay (into which it is unnecessary to go in a book like this).

Court etiquette

A circuit judge or a recorder should be addressed as "Your Honour". When addressing a district or deputy district judge it is always "Sir" or "Madam".

If the matter is in open court any address should be made standing. Only those persons actually addressing the court or giving evidence should speak.

Procedure

Whether the hearing is a fully contested trial or an interlocutory application, the basic procedure remains the same. The party who is bringing the claim or making the application will almost always begin. The applicant will briefly open the case by explaining to the judge what is being requested, the law to be relied on and what evidence may be called, if any. Where there are any preliminary points which the opposing party wishes to raise, for example challenging the court's jurisdiction to deal with the matter or attacking the validity of the process, these may be dealt with at this point. The judge will hear legal submissions and rule on the question before further time is wasted. If the matter then proceeds, the evidence will be called. All oral evidence must be given on oath, or by affirmation. (See also A. Dymond *Presenting Possession Proceedings*, chs. 5 and 6, Arden's Housing Library vol. 4, 1996.)

The evidence for the plaintiff will be called and this can be challenged in cross-examination. After the cross-examination is completed the witness may be re-examined by the lawyer on his or her own side. Re-examination is confined to matters arising out of cross-examination or for clarification of those issues. It is then the turn of the defendant whose evidence will be presented in the same way. The plaintiff goes first with all his or her evidence followed by the defendant.

Housing managers' evidence

Landlords in the social rented sector often rely heavily on the evidence of housing managers and surveyors (in-house or independent). Housing managers will be lay witnesses of fact and should be prepared to deal with issues such as tenants' complaints, action taken following complaint, the history of the dispute, and rent arrears if there is a counterclaim. If appearing as a lay witness, the manager must remember that any documents referred to must be brought to court and copies provided for the judge and the other party's lawyer. The witness must be able to attest that the document is genuine and so on. Each relevant document must have been disclosed in advance or the witness may be barred from referring to it or even producing it in evidence. If there is in any doubt about whether a document should be disclosed the manager should refer it to the legal department or solicitor for confirmation. In some cases the housing manager will require the housing file. However, if recourse is to be had to the housing file and it has not been disclosed in advance the other party would be en-titled to request disclosure of the file and may well seek an adjournment for consideration of its contents.

The most important role the housing manager may have is actually before trial. It is the keeping of clear records which frequently determines success or failure.

Experts' evidence

The role of an expert witness is clearly distinguished from that of a lay witness. The expert is required not only to deal with facts known to him or her but also to express an opinion on the interpretation of those facts in the context of the case before the court. For this reason, the expert evidence presented to the court must be independent and unbiased. The duties and responsibilites of the expert witness can be summarised as follows. An expert witness should:

• present evidence to the court which should be, and be seen to be, the independent product of the expert, uninfluenced as to form or content by the exigencies of litigation

• provide independent assistance to the court by way of objective opinion in relation to matters within his or her own area of expertise

• never assume the role of advocate

• state facts or substance upon which his or her opinion

is based
- not fail to consider material facts even where they detract from the conclusion
- make it clear when a particular question falls outside the scope of his or her expertise
- state his or her opinion as provisional if sufficient research has been impossible.

The duties imposed on an expert witness mean that even the factors damaging to his or her client's case must be taken into account. The expert must resist any inclination to become a member of the team (which has the attendant danger of the expert only giving those views which are favourable to his or her client).

In *Kenning v Eve Construction* [1989] 1 WLR 1189 the expert had written a report for disclosure together with a letter which expressed contrary views to those contained in the report (and contrary to his client's case). The court held that the party instructing the expert must either disclose all of the expert's opinion, including the damaging covering letter, or not rely on the expert at all.

If expert evidence will be required, it is imperative that the expert is instructed at an early stage and asked to review the problem as it progresses. It is false economy to permit a case to proceed to trial without assessing the merits fully. To leave the expert to the eleventh hour may result in a nasty shock and a large bill of cost if his or her view corresponds with what the plaintiff is saying.

Further assistance on the role of expert witnesses can be sought from P. Reddin *Dealing with Disrepair*, ch. 8.

Statutory nuisance in the magistrates' court

Statutory nuisance is heard in the magistrates' court and is a criminal matter. It will be dealt with either by a stipendiary magistrate (a full-time lawyer) alone, or by three lay magistrates. The manner in which a case is presented may be different according to whether the bench is familiar with the law or not.

The hearing will follow the same procedure as that in the county court. The main difference is the standard of proof which must be satisfied. In criminal cases it is proof beyond reasonable doubt, not the balance of probabilities as in the county court. This means that the defendant is entitled to have the benefit of the doubt. The rules on disclosure in the magistrates' court are less rigorous. It is not necessary for the defendant to prepare any written "defence" in advance, or to serve witness statements.

It is also important to remember that a criminal matter cannot be settled by the parties in the same manner as a civil action. It is usurping the court's jurisdiction to try to settle the case at the door of the court. This does not mean that the parties cannot come to an agreement, but this may for example require the defendant to enter a guilty plea, and the parties to present an agreed order for the works that are required.

Judgments and orders

At the end of a hearing the judge will announce his or her decision and record the terms of his or her judgment in an order. This often includes terms that the defendant (if on the losing side) pays monies to the plaintiff and carries out some works of repair, or abates the nuisance in a statutory nuisance case. It is essential that the housing manager has a copy of the judgment or order, as the responsibility for compliance will rest with his or her department. In some cases a penal notice will be attached to the order, which means that breach of the terms may result in imprisonment for contempt of court (see above p. 70).

Once an order is made it must be complied with. There is no scope for delay or compromise. If matters change after the date of the order, which means it cannot be complied with, that party will have to return to court to have the order varied.

Conclusion

The best way of dealing with litigation is to prevent it happening in the first place. If your case is weak and the tenant's strong, you have nothing to gain (and much to lose) by fighting, and a lot of good will to secure by responding promptly to ensure the tenant recovers the enjoyment of his or her home and that is, after all is said and done, the purpose of any social landlord.

APPENDIX I

CHECKLIST

The following is a summary and checklist for landlords and their housing managers. Adherence to this type of procedure may result in the landlord being able to respond swiftly when the law requires it to take action and being able to recognise *what* action is required. Where reasonableness is a factor, it is much less likely that it will be the landlord who will be found to have acted unreasonably. Tenants be generally happier, more comfortable and less inclined to legal action when the landlord has kept itself fully informed of the condition of its stock, of all complaints made and action taken.

- Before moving a tenant into a property, on a permanent or temporary basis, the **condition of the premises** must be checked for defects to the structure or exterior. The obligation to repair is firstly to *put* in repair.
- A programme of **regular inspection** of the stock for the purpose of identifying defects and potential problems is a right and duty of a landlord and will ensure the speedy remedy of defects for which it is liable.
- Any defects noticed as a result of inspection or as a

result of complaints made by tenants must be **logged immediately**. A tenant must prove notice or actual knowledge to found a legal action for disrepair. The absence of a logged complaint is only useful in negating notice if the procedure for the logging of complaints is accurate and reliable.

• If a defect is noted or reported, a **thorough search** should be conducted of the housing file for a record of any earlier complaint and/or action. Once legal proceedings are underway the rules of discovery require that tenants are shown the totality of the evidence.

• **Instruct** all officers, employees or agents about the procedure for logging of complaints with the appropriate person(s). It is no defence to argue that a complaint was not brought to the attention of those charged with responding.

• This should be followed by a prompt inspection of the property for purposes of **assessment** of the defect and its cause. If there is doubt – instruct an independent expert early.

• Having discovered the cause of the defect the housing manager must liaise with his or her legal advisers about the **tenant's entitlement** to the repair demanded – if in doubt don't sit on it – complaints do not go away.

• If the defect is one which requires urgent attention or threatens health and safety – consider the viability of **immediate remedy**.

• Repairs which are not urgent should still be prioritised. **Distinguish** between those repairs which *must* be carried out within a reasonable time and those which may be *desirable* but not legally enforceable and can safely be left for a longer term programme of works. Don't wait for the tenant to make an application to court for an interim injunction before considering the merits of the claim.

- Produce a schedule of repairs as against **target completion dates**. Then try to stick to them. They may be used by a tenant's adviser to demonstrate what is a reasonable time.
- If the tenant is not giving the landlord or its contractors **access** for the works, keep a clear record of attempts to gain access. These records can be crucial if the landlord hopes to rely on the tenant's unreasonable conduct.
- If attempts to gain access are without success, consider the legal action available to **compel** the tenant to permit access. Landlords must be seen to act reasonably and to have tried everything within their power to remedy any breach of the repairing obligation. There is nothing to be gained by waiting 12 months and then relying on the tenant's failure to permit the landlord to remedy its breach.
- Housing files and repair logs should be kept under **constant review** to ensure works which must be undertaken are ordered and then check that they have actually *been* undertaken and completed satisfactorily.
- Before relaxing, make a **further inspection** of the property to check the defect has in fact been remedied or the nuisance abated. This is particularly important where the landlord has engaged contractors not directly under its control.
- If legitimate legal action has been taken consider **settlement** by the offer of realistic compensation where it is clear that the tenant would succeed at trial.
- Before a landlord digs its heels in and prepares for a lengthy court battle, **reassess** the likelihood of success.

- If the case is going to proceed to a full trial – get your lawyers in early and provide them with **all of the relevant material**, regardless of whether it is detrimental.
- Consider who the **witnesses** will be and take statements from them while they still remember what happened.

APPENDIX II

COMPENDIUM OF DAMAGES AWARDS
IN DISREPAIR CASES

The selection given in this compendium of cases, both Court of Appeal and county court, give some indication of the "bench marks" for awards of damages for breach of the repairing obligation. Care must exercised before placing too much weight on precedents since each case will be judged on its own peculiar facts which may have aggravating or mitigating features. Account must also be taken of the effect of inflationary trends on the awards of damages, which are set out in chronological order. Bearing all this in mind, these decisions can be a very useful guide to the "going rate".

Taylor v Knowsley Borough Council (1985)
Résumé: Tenant of defendant authority in Liverpool; young, single man with relatives in area. Was without hot water for a period of 5 months from January, no ceiling light in living room for 3 months, some leaking through ceiling in bathroom causing some damp there for 8 months. No evidence of severe inconvenience. Carried out washing of clothes and bathing at relative's house.

Award: General damages were £92 i.e. £138 per annum.
(*Taylor v Knowsley Borough Council* (1985) 17 HLR 376 CA).

Yorston & Yorston v Crewfield Ltd and Festal International Ltd (1985)

Résumé: Private tenants, under a long lease, no children. Water seeping through ceiling when it rained, dry rot in the roof, without hot water for 2 months. Exposed holes in ceilings (from previous attempts to treat dry rot) which were not filled, causing increase in noise penetration. When it rained, the plaintiffs had to sleep in the living room. Clerkenwell County Court found that the conditions went beyond inconvenience and amounted to hardship over a period of 22 months. *Award:* General damages were £1,750 i.e. £954 per annum. (*Yorston & Yorston v Crewfield Ltd* and Festal International Ltd July 1985 Legal *Action*).

Hubble v London Borough of Lambeth (1985)

Résumé: Local authority tenants, married, no dependent children. Severe damp, draughty, cold living conditions, defective electric lighting, rotten floor boards. Tenant injured as a result of falling through floor. Disrepair extending over many years (the damp for 11 years). *Award:* General damages were £2,400. (*Hubble v London Borough of Lambeth* April 1986 *Legal Action* 50).

Downie v London Borough of Lambeth (1986)

Résumé: Local authority tenants, married, one dependent child. Extensive damp and general disrepair, leaking soil pipe, poor ventilation, inadequate kitchen. For 4 of the years when the family lived there the house

was considered to be unfit. The state of the house was described as "appalling".
Award: General damages were £4,000.
(*Downie v London Borough of Lambeth* July 1986 *Legal Action* 95).

Meah v London Borough of Tower Hamlets (1986)

Résumé: Local authority tenant with 3 young children. Leaking roof, penetrating damp through window frames, mould growing in most rooms (2 years), insect infestation in kitchen (3 months).
Award: General damages were £1,750.
(*Meah v London Borough of Tower Hamlets* October 1986 *Legal Action* 135).

Zone Properties v Painter (1987)

Résumé: Local authority tenant. Leaking roof causing water penetration initially in 1 room but spreading to others over 3 year period. Use of buckets by tenant kept premises habitable.
Award: General damages were £2,000.
(*Zone Properties v Painter* June 1987 *Legal Action* 21).

Felix v Karachristos and Jachni (1987)

Résumé: Private tenants. Wind and rain penetration, damp walls, faulty wiring and inefficient water heater over a period of 4 years and 3 months.
Award: General damages were £5,000.
(*Felix v Karachristos and Jachni* August 1987 *Legal Action* 17).

Rees v Davies (1987)

Résumé: Very bad conditions over 4 years. Leaking roof (so bad that ceiling fell), wet and decayed plaster, penetrating and rising damp. One room was unusable for 6 months. Works were carried out over 5 months whilst tenants were in occupation.

Award: General damages were £4,000.

(*Rees v Davies* September 1987 *Legal Action*).

Minchburn v Peck (1987)

General principle: Under the usual rules for the recovery of damages in contract, plaintiffs are under a duty to mitigate their losses. This is applied likewise to cases of landlord and tenant. Tenants are under a duty to mitigate by giving notice of the disrepair at an early stage. In this particular case, the failure affected the level of damages, in particular for discomfort and inconvenience, since the tenant could have improved his position by giving notice to the landlord. In reducing damages on this ground it is implicit that the landlord would have done something if given notice.

(*Minchburn v Peck* (1987) 20 HLR 392 CA).

Lubren v London Borough of Lambeth (1987)

Résumé: Local authority tenant. Disrepair began 1979. By 1984 the condition of the premises was considered "appalling". Cold and damp conditions, heating ineffective, windows jammed shut, no hot water.

Award: General damages were (a) in respect of the period 1979 to 1984, £4000 (i.e. £800 per annum) and (b) for the worst period commencing in 1984 to 1985, £500. (NB. The Court of Appeal dismissed the appeal against the award but said that the amount of £800 per annum

for the first period was probably too high and the amount
of £500 for the second period was probably too low).
(*Lubren v London Borough of Lambeth* (1987) 20 HLR
165 CA).

Sturolson & Co v Mauroux (1988)

Résumé: Private tenants were an elderly couple.
General disrepair, damp, faulty electrics, and without
constant hot water for heating and domestic purposes,
contrary to express covenant, limited to 6 years. It was
argued for the landlord that the tenants were only entitled to claim damages if they had taken reasonable
steps to mitigate their loss by carrying out at least some
of the repairs themselves. The judge in the lower court
found on the facts that they had not failed unreasonably to take steps and the Court of Appeal felt unable
to interfere. (N.B. In this case the judge took into
account, in assessing what would have been reasonable
to expect the tenants to do their physical vulnerability
and financial problems.)

Award: Damages were assessed under two heads: (i)
diminution in value to the tenants of their tenancy (as
a percentage of the tenants' rent for the period) and (ii)
damages for inconvenience etc. General damages were
£1,345 (including damages for breach of covenant to provide services) and £3,500 for inconvenience, distress etc.

General principle: In assessing damages, the correct
approach is to calculate the diminution in value of the
premises for the purpose of putting the tenants in the
position they would have been in had the breach not
occurred. In practice, where the tenants do not move
out of the property, diminution in value will often be
calculated by reference to the rent paid during the

period, plus an amount for inconvenience, discomfort and damage to health.
(*Sturolson & Co v Mauroux* (1988) 20 HLR 332).

Personal Representatives of Chiodi v de Marney (1988)

Résumé: Private tenant, single woman, aged 32 and in poor health. Defective heating, interruption of hot water supply, damp, cracks in walls and holes in the roof, over a three-and-a -half year period.

Award: General damages were £5,460 (i.e. £30 per week basedon diminution in value, plus a general award for inconvenience etc.) and £1,500 for ill-health. The level of damages was described by the Court of Appeal as "high – that is to say, at the very top of what at this time could in my view be regarded as a proper award on these facts."

General principle: "The correct approach is to calculate the diminution in value of the premises for the purpose of putting the tenant in the position he would have been in had the breach not occurred. This will normally involve the calculation of costs of alternative accommodation, the cost of redecoration, and an amount of compensation for discomfort, inconvenience and ill-health etc. will be added where appropriate."
(*Personal Representatives of Chiodi v de Marney* (1988) 21 HLR 6).

Jones v Derval Dampcoursing (1990)

Résumé: Private tenant. Repeated failure of damp proof course, leaving occupier unable to decorate for 4 years and during this time living in "a miserable state".

Award: General damages were £2,500.
(*Jones v Derval Dampcoursing* (1990) 8 CLR 128).

Thompson v Birmingham City Council (1990)

Résumé: Local authority tenant, single man. Acute rising damp which lasted over 4 years.
Award: General damages were £4,500 (i.e. £17 per week).
(*Thompson v Birmingham City Council* September 1990 *Legal Action*).

Televantos v McCulloch (1990)

Résumé: Private tenant, single woman, middle-aged. Extensive disrepair throughout property; 3 years of disrepair followed by a period of up to 1 year during which extensive works of repair were carried out while she remained in the property, at great inconvenience to her. Work required was substantial structural alteration, re-positioning of water tanks etc.
Award: General damages were £1,700.
(*Televantos v McCulloch* (1990) 23 HLR 412).

Berry v Avrisons Co Ltd (1990)

Résumé: Private tenant, single man. Dampness, disrepair and interrupted hot water supply over 4 year period.
Award: General damages were £5,000.
(*Berry v Avrisons Co Ltd* March 1991 *Legal Action*).

Stratton and Porter v Arakpo and London Borough of Southwark (1990)

Résumé: Private tenants then becoming local authority tenants after the council took over management. Until 1987 premises had been almost derelict, a health hazard and unsafe. In that year premises taken over by the council which carried out some works but by 1990 the property was again found to be unfit for human habitation and prejudicial to health.

Award: General damages were £1,000 per annum inconvenience and ill-health plus diminution in value of 90 per cent of the rent.

(*Stratton and Porter v Arakpo and London Borough of Southwark* June 1991 *Legal Action*).

Trustees of Calthorpe Edgbaston Estate v Routledge (1990)

Résumé: Private tenant. Extensive disrepair, permeating dampness. 6 years' discomfort and inconvenience, 3 years' personal injury.

Award: General damages were £4,186.

(*Trustees of Calthorpe Edgbaston Estate v Routledge* December 1991 *Legal Action*).

London Borough of Lambeth v Williams (1991)

Résumé: Local authority tenant. Single woman with 6 year-old daughter. Water penetration into living room over 4 year period.

Award: General damages were £700 per annum plus £500 per annum diminution in value.

(*London Borough of Lambeth v Williams* December 1991 *Legal Action*).

Sullivan v Johnson (1991)

Résumé: Private tenant, aged 96 years. Property found to be appalling, with penetrating damp, collapsed ceilings, rising damp and rot.

Award: General damages were £300 per annum for the period between 1977-84, and for the period 1984-91 when conditions were at the very top end of the bracket for which damages for disrepair and discomfort are awarded, £1,000 per annum.

(*Sullivan v Johnson* March 1992 *Legal Action* 13).

Cook v Horford Investment Ltd and Mohammed Taj (1992)

Résumé: Private tenant, single man. Serious disrepair with water penetrating through roof and defective windows for period of 3 years.

Award: General damages were £4,500 (inconvenience and ill-health) plus £1,958 (diminution in value of rent by 50 per cent).

(*Cook v Horford Investment Ltd and Mohammed Taj* September 1992 *Legal Action*).

Lasky v Webb (1993)

Résumé: Private tenant, married with 2 young children. Two-storey house, occupied for 8 months. Roof leaked, windows were rotten, defective electric installations, extensive general disrepair. Premises had been declared unfit for human habitation.

Award: General damages were £1,000 (for inconvenience and ill-health for the 8 months) plus £1,052 (for diminution of 80 per cent of the rent also for the 8 month period) i.e. £3,078 per annum.

(*Lasky v Webb* March 1993 *Legal Action*).

London Borough of Lambeth v Guerreo (1992)

Résumé: Local authority tenant, married with 3 children. Premises in disrepair since 1981. In 1984 an environmental health officer served public health service notice as a result of severe damp and mould growth. The period of disrepair was 7 years.

Award: General damages: £8,000 (inconvenience and ill-health) plus £6,000 (diminution in value of rent) i.e. £2,000 per annum.

(*London Borough of Lambeth v Guerreo* (1992) March 1993 *Legal Action*).

Parish v Leslie (1994)

Résumé: Private sector tenant with 2 children. Rented house for 8 months. Roof leaked, rising damp, drainage system in disrepair, ineffective heating system, gas fire not working.

Award: General damages were £800 (inconvenience) plus £1,200 (diminution in value of rent by 50 per cent).

(*Parish v Leslie* August 1994 *Legal Action*).

Hallett v London Borough of Camden (1994)

Résumé: Local authority tenant. Cracks to walls and ceilings, defective sash windows which caused premises to be draughty. The court found that the cracking of the ceilings was so minor as not to be actionable at all and described the defective windows as minor.

Award: General damages were £750 for a period of just over 2 years.

(*Hallett v London Borough of Camden* August 1994 *Legal Action*).

Dadd v Christian Action (Enfield) Housing Association (1994)

Résumé: A single parent with 2 young children lived in a 2 bedroom flat for two and a half years. For the whole of the period of the tenancy there was an infestation of rats, dampness in the kitchen and the heating and hot water were defective.

Award: General damages were £1,300 per annum (inconvenience and distress); damages for diminution in value were £790 per annum (40 per cent of the rent); special damages were £1,950. Total: £7,476.

(*Dadd v Christian Action (Enfield) Housing Association* March 1994 *Legal Action*).

London Borough of Lambeth v Defreitas (1994)

Résumé: The local authority had begun a possession action on the basis of rent arrears and the tenant counterclaimed for damages for disrepair. There was penetrating damp caused by defective external rainwater pipes, intermittent failure of heating and hot water and leaking radiators. For a period of 8 years there was severe damp affecting the living rooms of the flat.

Award: General damages were £12 per week for the first 4 years when tenant was alone and disrepair was less serious, £25 per week for the last 5 years when tenant had 2 children and the damp had become serious; £500 damages for inconvenience of temporary removal while works being carried out; £1,200 injury to health (respiratory infection, anxiety and depression exacerbated by disrepair); £878 special damages; and interest. Total: £12,785.

(*London Borough of Lambeth v Defreitas* March 1994 *Legal Action*).

Lewin v London Borough of Brent (1995)

Résumé: Council tenant purchased his council flat under the right to buy scheme. His lease expressly required the council to keep in repair the common parts and curtilage and to provide caretaking, rubbish collection and cleaning. For a period of 6 years the service areas were in disrepair; the estate was not kept clean and the rubbish was not collected.

Award: General damages were £500 for 2 years when sewers had overflowed and a further £300 per annum for the remainder of the time; £1,500 diminution in value; £375 special damages.

(*Lewin v London Borough of Brent* March 1995 *Current Law Weekly*).

London Borough of Brent v Carmel (sued as Murphy) (1995)

Résumé: The tenant first complained of dampness and a defective central heating system in 1981. The condition of her home became progressively worse and from 1986 onwards was "appalling and intolerable". The home was so cold and damp that the tenant and her two children had to sleep in outdoor clothes. For part of that time they had to share 1 bedroom.

Award: Damages for discomfort and inconvenience were £14,000; damages for loss of value were 30 per cent of rent from 1986-87 and 50 per cent from 1988-93; special damages were £19,320. The Court of Appeal said this award at first instance could not be described as manifestly excessive or wrong in principle.

(*London Borough of Brent v Carmel* (1995) 28 HLR, CA).

Ali v Birmingham City Council (1995)

Résumé: The tenants' Victorian traditional terraced house was in serious disrepair from before March 1987. Conditions deteriorated until April 1992, when they were provided with "temporary accommodation" pending works. They were not able to return until January 1993, but the remedial works were still incomplete and were not concluded until November 1994. The primary problem was dampness, rising dampness through the floors and penetrating damp through the walls.

Award: General damages were £15,750; special damages were £750.

(*Ali v Birmingham City Council* June 1995 *Legal Action* 22).

London Borough of Newham v Hewitt (1995)

Résumé: In 1989 the council installed central heating in the tenant's home in place of an underfloor system. The radiators in the bedrooms and hallway failed to work at all and 1 of the 3 radiators in the living room was defective. The problem continued for 4 years, during which his home was so cold that the frail tenant in his late fifties wore his overcoat in the living room and went to bed in his clothes.

Award: General damages were £4,000.

(*London Borough of Newham v Hewitt* June 1995 *Legal Action*).

APPENDIX III

DEFENDING A REPAIRS CLAIM

Sample pleadings

The following is an example of a defence to a council tenant's claim for damages for breach of the repairing obligation. The example is the local authority's response to a typical Particulars of Claim in such an action; the hypothetical facts are as follows:

The tenant has lived in a two-bedroom council flat with her 2 young children since September 1993. In October 1994 she made a written complaint to her local housing office that the premises were damp and had been that way from about November 1993. She asserts that she had made earlier verbal complaints. There were no previous complaints either oral or in writing recorded by the local authority, which was not aware of any damp at the premises prior to the tenant's complaint. Since first complaining the tenant had arranged to let contractors in to the premises to inspect and carry out works but at the arranged time was not present at the premises. Various attempts were made to gain access but this was not possible until October 1995, at which time some works were completed. The tenant engaged a surveyor who reported that the damp was due to water penetrating through the window frames which were defective, and possible rising damp due to deterioration of the damp proof course. The local authority's expert agreed that the windows were defective but claimed that this had been remedied in 1995 and that the dampness was due to condensation exacerbated by the tenant's use of the premises. The tenant is in arrears with her rent.

In the Central London County
Case No 53426

Between:
Lucy Smith
(Plaintiff)

– and –

The London Borough of Harrington
(Defendants)

PARTICULARS OF CLAIM

1. By an agreement in writing, dated 21st September 1993 (hereinafter referred to as the "Agreement") the Defendants granted to the Plaintiff a secure tenancy of premises known as and situate at 34 Gravesend Street, London (the "premises") at a weekly rent of £34.00. The premises comprise a two bedroom maisonette and have at all material times since September 1993 been occupied by the Plaintiff and her two children Dorothy (born 18th April 1990) and James (born 20th July 1992).

---

2. It was an express term of the tenancy that the Defendants would keep in repair and proper working order the structure of the premises.

3. Section 11 of the Landlord and Tenant Act 1985 applies to the tenancy.

4. It was an implied term of the tenancy that the Defendants would keep in repair the structure and exterior of the premises and the building in which the premises were situated, and keep in repair and proper working order the installations therein for the supply of water, gas and electricity, and for sanitation. space heating and heating water, and such installations as directly or indirectly serve the premises and form part of any part of a building which is owned by or under the control of the Plaintiff.

5. Further, or alternatively, it was an implied term of the Agreement that the Defendants would not derogate from their grant of the premises to the Plaintiff.

6. Further and in the further alternative, the Defendants owe a duty to take reasonable care that the Plaintiff and her children are reasonably safe from personal injury or damage to their property.

7. The Defendants are in breach of the said terms pleaded herein above:

PARTICULARS OF BREACH
i. from about November 1993 the premises have been damp and unsightly, with damp patches apparent around the windows;

ii. from about November 1993 the premises have suffered from rising dampness which has discoloured the wallpaper, and the plaster is cracked;

iii. from the outset of the tenancy the window frames have been defective with draughty gaps;

iv. the cills of the aforementioned windows are rotten due to the accumulation of water upon them.

8. By reason of the matters pleaded under sub-paragraphs i. to iv. inclusive of paragraph 7 the Defendants have derogated from their grant.

9. At all material times the Defendants have had notice of the matters complained of:

PARTICULARS OF NOTICE
a) on occasions too numerous to particularise herein the Plaintiff has complained to her neighbourhood office of the damp;

b) without prejudice to the generality of the foregoing the Plaintiff wrote to the Defendants on 14th October 1994 setting out the defects at the premises.

10. By reason of the matters complained of the Plaintiff has suffered loss and damage:

PARTICULARS OF LOSS AND DAMAGE
a) the value of the tenancy to the Plaintiff has been diminished;

b) since about November 1993 the premises have been cold and damp as the result of the said windows being defective and the damp proof course having deteriorated;

c) by reasons of the condition of the premises the Plaintiff has been too embarrassed to invite friends to her home;

PARTICULARS OF SPECIAL DAMAGE

a) the damp has ruined clothes, food and furnishings belonging to the Plaintiff and her children. A full schedule of such losses will be provided in due course;

b) for the duration of the tenancy the Plaintiff has suffered stress as a result of the defects pleaded here- in above;

c) the Plaintiff has expended additional monies on heating the premises due to the damp and draughty windows.

11. Further, the Plaintiff claims interest upon any sums found to be due to her, pursuant to section 69 of the County Courts Act 1984, at such rate and for such periods as the court considers just.

AND the Plaintiff claims:

1. an order for specific performance of the Defendants' obligations;

2. damages in excess of £5,000;

3. the aforesaid interest.

Dated this 10th day of June 1996

In the Central London County Court
Case No. 53426

Between:
Lucy Smith
(Plaintiff)

– and –

The London Borough of Harrington
(Defendants)

DEFENCE AND COUNTERCLAIM

1. Paragraphs 1 to 5 of the Particulars of Claim are admitted. *[NB. Admissions should only be made in respect of matters which are factually correct and those assertions of law which are undeniable. An admission can only be withdrawn later with the permission of the court.]*

2. Save that it is admitted that the Defendants owe a duty to take reasonable care that the Plaintiff and her children are safe from personal injury where that injury may be caused by a defect, paragraph 6 of the Particulars of Claim is denied. *[NB. The Plaintiff here is relying on the Defective Premises Act. However that liability on the landlord only arises when there is a relevant defect and not to the broad extent that has been pleaded in the Particulars of Claim.]*

3. Paragraph 7 of the Particulars of Claim is denied in its entirety. Without prejudice to the generality of the foregoing it is specifically denied that the premises suffer from penetrating dampness. The Defendants

aver that any dampness which may have been present at the premises was caused by condensation resulting from the Plaintiff's failure to use the premises in a tenant-like manner. In particular, the Plaintiff sealed up the windows thereby preventing any air from circulating and failed to use the heating system which was provided. *[NB. If there is evidence from the landlord's expert that the cause of the damp is condensation which is not caused or exacer-bated by disrepair then the positive assertion to that effect should be included here to the extent that condensation is not a defect which comes within section 11.]*

4. Paragraph 8 of the Particulars of Claim is denied.

5. Save that it is admitted that the Defendants received a letter from the Plaintiff in or about October 1994 in relation solely to dampness at the premises, Paragraph 9 of the Particulars of Claim is denied. Without prejudice to the generality of the foregoing it is specifically denied that the Plaintiff gave notice of any defects, as alleged or at all, before October 1994. The Defendants aver that on receiving notice of the alleged dampness, the Defendants attempted to carry out an inspection of the premises for the purposes of identifying any defects for which the Defendants may be responsible, and for remedying the same within a reasonable time.

6. It was an express and/or implied term of the tenancy that the Plaintiff would permit the Defendants or their servants, agents or contractors, entry to the premises for the purposes of inspection and repair. In breach of the said term the Plaintiff repeatedly denied access to the Defendants' contractors. The

said contractors were engaged to inspect the premises and to carry out remedial works, if such were required on 23rd October 1994. The Defendants aver that such defects which may have been present at the premises would have been remedied within a reasonable time of the Defendants receiving notice of the same, but for the Plaintiff's failure to permit access. In relation to the premises it is denied that the Defendants are in breach of the terms pleaded or at all.

7. Paragraphs 10 and 11 of the Particulars of Claim are not admitted and the Plaintiff is put to strict proof of the matters pleaded therein. If, which is not admitted, the Plaintiff did suffer any loss or damage the Defendants will assert that this was as a result of the Plaintiff's refusal to permit the Defendants' contractors to enter the premises to inspect and/or carry out works. Further or alternatively, in the premises, the Plaintiff has failed to take any steps to mitigate her loss.

8. Save as has been expressly admitted or not admitted herein above, the Defendant denies each and every allegation contained in the Particulars of Claim as if the same were set out and traversed *seriatim*.

9. Further or alternatively, the Defendants are entitled to set-off the sums herein counterclaimed in diminution or extinction of any sums found to be due to the Plaintiff.

COUNTERCLAIM
10. The Defendants repeat their Defence herein.

11. The Plaintiff is and has been, at all material times,

the freehold owner of the said premises. By an agreement in writing dated 11th September 1993, the Defendants let to the Plaintiff, the premises, on a weekly tenancy commencing 11th September at the rent of £14.46 per week.

12. In breach of the said agreement, the Plaintiff has failed and/or refused to pay the said rent. In the premises, the Plaintiff is indebted to the Defendants in the sum of £1,245.89. A full copy of the rent account relating to the premises is appended herewith. [NB. Append to the pleadings a computer print out of the rent arrears.]

13. Further, the Defendants claim interest pursuant to section 69 of the County Courts Act 1984, at such rate and on such amount as the court thinks fit.

AND the Defendants Counterclaim:

1. the sum of £1,245.89;

2. the aforesaid interest pursuant to section 69 of the County Courts Act 1984;

3. costs.

Dated this 4th day of July 1996

The landlord may wish to issue proceedings, particularly to gain access. The following is a hypothetical example of the application by a local authority required for an injunction, and the particulars of claim in an action for access.

APPLICATION FOR
AN ACCESS INJUCTION

In the Central London County Court
Case No. 53426

Between:
The London Borough of Harrington
(Plaintiffs)

– and –

Lucy Smith
(Defendant)

I wish to apply for an order that:

1. the Defendant do give to the Plaintiffs, its servants or agents, access to the premises for the purpose of inspecting the same and carrying out the works that are required, at 10.30 am on Monday the 7th July 1996, or at such other time as the court considers just;

2. the costs of this application be the Plaintiffs' in any event.
The grounds of this application are set out in the Affidavit of Mr Tryhard, sworn on the 4th day of March 1996.

Dated this 4th day of March 1996

[The application must be accompanied by an affidavit in support setting out and verifying the facts and containing a statement of belief that the Defendant will continue to refuse to permit access unless a court order is obtained.]

In the Central London County Court
Case No. 53426

Between:

The London Borough of Harrington
(Plaintiffs)

– and –

Lucy Smith
(Defendant)

PARTICULARS OF CLAIM

1. At all material times the Plaintiffs have been the freehold owner of premises known as and situate at 34 Gravesend Street, London, (the "premises"). Since 21st September 1993 the Defendant has been the secure tenant of the Plaintiffs.

2. The Defendant's tenancy agreement was in writing, dated 21st September 1993 (the "Agreement") upon the terms, conditions and covenants contained therein. The Plaintiffs will rely on the Agreement at trial for its full terms and legal effect.

3. By clause 1.8 of the said Agreement the Defendant covenanted to give access to the premises to the Plaintiffs and/or the Plaintiffs' servants or agents, upon the Plaintiffs giving 48 hours notice, for the purposes of inspecting the condition of the premises and carrying out any works that are required.

4. Further or alternatively, it was an implied term of the agreement that the Defendant would give access to the Plaintiffs and/or the Plaintiffs' servants or

agents, for the purposes of inspecting the condition of the premises and carrying out any works that are required, upon the Plaintiffs giving reasonable notice.

5. On 14th October 1994 the Defendant complained to the Plaintiffs that the premises were damp and in disrepair. Further to this complaint the Plaintiffs, by its officer Mr Tryhard, wrote to the Defendant, by letter dated 22nd October 1994, to arrange a date upon which the Plaintiffs' officers could inspect the premises and carry out whatever works were considered to be necessary. An appointment was made for the 23rd October 1994 but on arrival at the premises the Plaintiffs' officers were refused access.

6. Further, by letters dated 14th, 20th, 28th November 1994 and 17th January 1995 the Plaintiffs requested access to the premises.

7. In breach of the said express and/or implied terms the Defendant has refused and continues to refuse to give access to the Plaintiffs, its servants or agents.

8. In the premises the Plaintiffs claim an injunction requiring the Defendant to give to the Plaintiffs, its servants or agents, access to the premises for the purpose of inspecting the same and carrying out the works that are required, at 10.30 am on Monday the 7th July 1996, or at such other time as the court considers just.

AND the Plaintiffs claim:

(i) A mandatory injunction requiring the Defendant to give to the Plaintiffs, its servants or agents, access to the premises for the purpose of inspecting the same and carrying out the works that are required, at 10.30 am on Monday the 7th July 1996, or at such other time as the court considers just.

Dated this 4th day of March 1996

APPENDIX IV

GLOSSARY OF TERMS

This glossary provides a concise explanation of the meaning of some of the more legalistic and technical terms used in the guide.

Affidavit
– a formal, written statement by a witness made on oath.

Assured tenancy
– a tenancy that fulfils the requirements of the Housing Act 1988. An assured tenancy can be granted only from 15 January 1989 by landlords who are either housing associations or in the private sector.

Burden of proof
– the obligation on a party to prove a fact in issue between the parties. The burden of proof in civil proceedings is "on the balance of probabilities".

Common law
– a phrase generally used to describe the law arising not from statutory sources but from case-law.

Covenant
– a clause in a tenancy agreement under which either the landlord or the tenant promises to act in a certain way; for example, to carry out repairs or not to be a nuisance to neighbours.

Cross-examination
– the questioning of a witness by the opposing party.

Directions
– an order by the court setting out the procedural steps which are to be gone through prior to the trial of a case, and providing a time scale within which the steps are to be carried out.

Discovery
– the production by each party of all documents which may be relevant to the issues of the case.

Evidence in chief
– the evidence given by a witness in support of the case to be made.

Ex parte
– an application to the court, which is made urgently and without the opposing party in the litigation being informed that the hearing is to take place. (Abbreviation: ex p.)

Fixed term tenancy
– a tenancy which is granted for a fixed period, for example, six months, or one year, or 99 years. (Compare periodic tenancy, below.)

Further and better particulars
– if alleged facts set out in a pleading are too general, a request by the opposing party may be made to expand on those allegations in a formal request for further and better particulars. (See also pleadings, below.)

Hearsay
– an out of court statement tendered in court as evidence of the truth of its contents. Hearsay is essentially "second-hand" evidence.

Injunction
– an order of the court that a person should carry out certain acts or should refrain from carrying out certain acts.

Interlocutory
– an interim order in a case that is made before the final trial and judgment, most often used with injunctions.

Negligence
– a duty of care under common law which may be imposed where there is no contractual or statutory liability.

Notice seeking possession
– the notice served by the landlord on a secure or assured tenancy, prior to commencing possession proceeding. It must specify the grounds on which possession is sought against the tenant.

Notice to quit
– formal notice by a landlord determining a periodic tenancy of a tenant who does not have security of tenure.

Nuisance
– the interference by one occupier of land with another's occupation of his or her own land.

Particulars of claim
– the formal statement of the plaintiff's case which must be served with the summons for possession.

Periodic tenancy
– a tenancy which does not have a fixed time-span from the outset but which is set in terms of a regular rental payment, for example, monthly or weekly.

Plaintiff
– the person bringing the case, i.e. in possession proceedings, the landlord.

Pleadings
– the formal statements to the court by each party of the facts of the case upon which they intend to rely at trial.

Quiet enjoyment
– the right of tenants to occupy their homes without interference from their landlords. A right to quiet enjoyment is automatically implied into all tenancy agreements.

Re-examination
– questions by the party who called a witness in response to matters arising out of cross-examination.

Secure tenancy
– a tenancy that fulfils the requirements of the Housing Act 1985, granted by local authorities or, before 15 January 1989, housing associations.

Specific performance
– an order of the court that a particular term of a contract should be performed, for example, to carry out repairs; or to desist from behaviour which is a breach of a tenancy agreement.

Unless order
– an order of the court requiring a party to proceedings to act within a certain time. It includes the provision that if the act is not carried out, the party will be prevented from continuing to pursue or defend the case.

Witness statements
– written statements by the trial witnesses setting out all the facts concerned in the evidence which they are to give in court. The statements are exchanged by the parties in advance of the trial.

CUMULATIVE INDEX

Abandoned premises
  conditions for security of
    tenure, 1:53-54
  notice to quit, 1:110-111
Absence from premises
  conditions for security of
    tenure, 1:48-49
  prolonged, 1:48-49
Accelerated procedure
  possession proceedings,
    1:108, 4:114
Access
  **neighbouring land, to,
    5:115-116**
Accident
  inevitable, as defence to
    private nuisance action,
    3:21-22
Accommodation
  disabled, for, 1:80
  elderly, for, 1:19-20
  employment related, 1:76-77,
    4:41-42
  essential for job, 1:24-25
  homeless persons, for, 1:34-35
    1:42
  hostel. See Hostel
    accommodation
  information about
    applications, 2:58-59
  job mobility, 1:35-36
  pending works, 1:37, 1:77-78,
    4:40-41

  shared, 1:45-46
  sheltered, 1:81
  special needs, 1:80-81
  tied, 1:24, 1:88, 4:34-35
Adjournment of possession
  proceedings. See Possession
    proceedings
Affidavit
  evidence, 4:71-72
  meaning, 4:154
  summary possession, 4:116
Agent
  repairs,
    liability for, 5:10-11
    notice relating to, 5:33-35
Agreement
  surrender, to, 1:125
  tenancy,
    assured tenancy, 2:54-55
    breach of, as ground for
      possession, 3:60-61
    changing terms of, 2:50-55
    covenant, meaning, 2:99
    fixed term tenancy, 2:54
    harassment, prevention of,
      3:84-87
    inspection of disrepair,
      preparing for, 6:73
    periodic tenancy, 2:54-55
    secure tenancy, 2:50-54
    termination of, 4:8-13
Agricultural holdings
  tenancy of, 1:37, 1:40

Entries in this volume appear in bold.
1. *Security of Tenure* 2. *Tenants' Rights* 3. *Nuisance and Harassment*
4. *Presenting Possession Proceedings* 5. *Repairs and Maintenance*
6. *Dealing with Disrepair*

Agricultural land
  assured tenancy, exception to,
    1:40
Allocation of housing
  information about, 2:57-58
  secure tenants, information
    to, 2:62
  suitable alternative
    accommodation, 1:91-92
Ancillary rights of tenants
  summary, 2:3-4
Animals
  disease carrying, 6:55
  private nuisance, as, 3:16
Annoyance
  assured tenant, grounds for
    possession against, 1:88
  evidence, 1:72
  letter to tenant causing, 1:133
  meaning, 1:71
  neighbours, complaints from,
    1:72
  nuisance and, 3:61-63
  possession proceedings,
    generally, 4:106-109
  proof of annoyance, 4:39
  return date, 4:110
  undertakings, 4:110-112
  witness statement, 4:110
  secure tenant, grounds for
    possession against, 1:70-73
  those who live with tenant,
    caused by, 1:71
  visitors, caused by, 1:71
Appeals
  **compensation orders, relating
    to, 5:102**
  **environmental protection,
    relating to, 5:102**
  possession procedure,
    4:136-137
Application to set aside
  possession order, 1:123-124
Asbestos
  complaints relating to, 5:59-60
  removal contractors, 6:52-53

use of, 6:52-53
Asphalt
  description of, 6:34-35
Assignment
  assured tenancy, of, 2:44-46
  enforcement of right of,
    2:28-29
  exchange, by way of,
    consent, grounds for
      refusing, 2:36-39
    generally, 2:35
    landlord's written consent,
      2:35-36
  generally, 1:8, 2:31
  potential successor, to, 2:32-33
  proof of, 2:33-34
  secure tenancy, of,
    exchange, assignment by
      way of, 2:35-39
    generally, 2:32
    mutual exchange, 2:35-39
    potential successor, to,
      2:32-33
    proof of assignment, 2:33-34
    property transfer order,
      2:32
    successor assignee, seeking
      possession against, 2:34-35
  statutory periodic tenancy,
    2:46
Assured shorthold tenancy
  county court, accelerated
    procedure in, 1:108
  features, 1:106-107
  hostel accommodation, 1:116
  nature of, 1:105
  new shorthold, 1:107
  possession, 1:107, 4:113-114
  probationary tenancy, 3:44-45
  purposes, 1:106
Assured tenancy
  assignment of, 2:44-2:46
  change of landlord, 1:42
  conditions, 1:44
  consultation with assured
    tenants, 2:75-77

Entries in this volume appear in bold.
1. *Security of Tenure* 2. *Tenants' Rights* 3. *Nuisance and Harassment*
4. *Presenting Possession Proceedings* 5. *Repairs and Maintenance*
6. *Dealing with Disrepair*

exceptions,
  agricultural holdings,
    tenancy of, 1:40
  agricultural land, tenancy
    of, 1:40
  business tenancy, 1:40
  crown tenancy, 1:41
  exempt landlord, 1:41
  high rateable values,
    tenancy of premises
    with, 1:39
  holiday lets, 1:40
  homeless person, 1:42
  licensed premises, 1:40
  long leaseholder, 1:40
  resident landlord, 1:41
  student lets, 1:40
  tenancy created before
    commencement of Act,
    1:39
  tenants with other classes
    of protection, 1:41
  forfeiture of, 1:66
  generally, 1:29
  lodgers, 2:47
  meaning, 2:99, 3:99, 4:154
  nature of, 1:38-39
  possession, grounds of,
    annoyance, 1:88
    breach of term of tenancy,
      1:87
    deterioration of dwelling-
      house, 1:88
    discretionary grounds,
      1:86-88
    furniture, deterioration of,
      1:88
    generally, 1:83
    holiday letting out of
      season, 1:84
    inherited tenancy, 1:85-86
    landlord's works, 1:84-85
    mandatory grounds, 1:84-86
    ministers of religion, 1:84
    mortgaged property, 1:84
    nuisance, 1:88

  rent arrears, 1:86, 1:87
  returning home owner, 1:84
  specimen form of order,
    4:150-151
  student letting, 1:84
  suitable alternative
    accommodation, 1:87
  tied accommodation, 1:88
  rights of tenants,
    generally, 2:5-6
    tenants' guarantees, 2:6-7
  shorthold. *See* Assured
    shorthold tenancy
  subletting, 2:46
  succession,
    common law, at, 2:23-24
    contractual succession
      clauses, 2:26-30
    generally, 2:23
    Housing Act 1988, under,
      2:24-25
    who is successor, 2:25
    who succeeds, 2:25
  suitable alternative
    accommodation,
    comparison with local
      authority practice, 1:94
    furniture, 1:94
    generally, 1:93
    local authority certificate,
      1:93
    location, 1:95
    reluctant tenants, 1:94-95
    suitability, 1:93-94
  tenancy agreement, 2:54-55

Basements
  damp-proofing, 6:19
Behaviour of perpetrator
  private nuisance and, 3:18
Bituminous materials
  description of, 6:34-35
Breach
  other term, of, reasonableness
    and, 1:102-103
  repairs, relating to. *See*

Entries in this volume appear in bold.
1. *Security of Tenure* 2. *Tenants' Rights* 3. *Nuisance and Harassment*
4. *Presenting Possession Proceedings* 5. *Repairs and Maintenance*
6. *Dealing with Disrepair*

Repairs and maintenance
Brick
   description of, 6:26
   external walls,
      cavity brickwork, 6:10
      solid brickwork, 6:10
   footings, 6:12
Building
   **Act of 1984, local authority
      powers under, 5:105**
   diagnosing defects, 6:163-167
   diagrams, 6:147-162
   disrepair. *See* Disrepair
   repairs. *See* Repairs and
      maintenance
Burden of proof
   meaning, 4:154
Bushes
   disrepair caused by, 6:55-56
Business tenancy
   assured tenancy, exclusion
      from, 1:40
   secure tenancy, exclusion
      from, 1:38

Camera
   inspection of disrepair, use
      for, 6:76
Causation
   **compensation awards,
      assessment of, 5:101-102**
Change of landlord
   assured tenancy, 1:42
   secure tenancy, 1:42
Charity
   secure tenant, grounds for
      possession against, 1:79
Chartered Institute of Housing
   *Housing Management
      Standards Manual,* 6:122
Climate. *See* Temperature and
   climate
Closing speeches
   possession proceedings, 4:81
Cockroaches
   complaints relating to,

5:60-63
   private nuisance, as, 3:17
Codes of practice
   disrepair, priorities in dealing
      with, 6:119-120
Cohabitees
   rights of, 1:111-112
Commencing possession
   proceedings. *See*
   Possession proceedings
Commission for Racial Equality
   racial harassment, meaning,
      3:70
Committal proceedings
   meaning, 4:154
Committees
   representation on, 2:76-77
Common law
   meaning, 3:99
   public nuisance, 3:23-24
   succession at, 2:10, 2:23-24
Common parts
   damage to, 1:74
   inspection of disrepair,
      preparing for, 6:73
   repair, liability for, 5:22-24
Compensation
   improvements, for, 5:125
   orders,
      appeals, 5:102
      causation, 5:101-102
      **levels of compensation,
         5:101**
      power to make, 5:100-101
Complaints
   damp, relating to,
      condensation damp, 5:56-57
      generally, 5:53
      penetrating damp, 5:53-55
      rising damp, 5:55-56
   neighbours, from, 1:72
   nuisance, relating to, 3:39-40
Compulsory competitive
   tendering
   local authority, by, 2:89
   nuisance and, 3:43-44

Entries in this volume appear in bold.
1. *Security of Tenure* 2. *Tenants' Rights* 3. *Nuisance and Harassment*
4. *Presenting Possession Proceedings* 5. *Repairs and Maintenance*
6. *Dealing with Disrepair*

Concrete
  description of, 6:30
  reinforced,
    foundations, 6:13
    frame, 6:21
Condensation
  complaints relating to, 5:56-57
  from inside, 6:45
  interstitial, 6:46
Conditions for security of
tenure
  abandonment, 1:53-54
  assured tenancy, 1:44
  dwelling-house, 1:44
  gaining possession, 1:55
  generally, 1:43
  let as separate dwelling,
    meaning, 1:45-46
    separate, meaning, 1:45
    shared accomodation,
      1:45-46
  lodgers,
    generally, 1:51
    illegal occupation, 1:52-53
    loss of security of tenure,
      1:51-52
  residence condition, 1:43,
    1:46-51
  secure tenancy, 1:43-44
  subletting,
    generally, 1:51
    illegal occupation, 1:52-53
    loss of security of tenure,
      1:51-52
  surrender, 1:53-54
  use as home,
    absence from premises,
      1:48-49
    prolonged absence, 1:48-49
    residence condition, 1:46-51
    two homes, 1:49-51
Consent order
  possession proceedings,
    4:126-129
Consolidation
  meaning, 4:154

possession proceedings,
    4:51-52
Construction materials. *See*
  Materials of construction
Consultation
  assured tenants, with,
    2:75-77
  committees, representation on,
    generally, 2:77
    housing associations,
      2:78
    local authorities, 2:77
  housing action trust,
    declaration of, 2:93
  housing association,
    sale tenanted to, 2:92
    sale with vacant
      possession, 2:93
  local authority,
    redevelopment by, 2:94
  other forms, 2:77-79
  rent levies for tenants' funds,
    2:79
  secure tenants, with,
    acquisition by new
      landlord, 2:74-75
    basic requirement, 2:65
    generally, 2:65
    housing action trust, 2:73-74
    large scale voluntary
      transfers, 2:71-72
    managing agents, use of,
      2:69-71
    matters requiring
      consultation, 2:66-69
    method of consultation,
      2:65-66
    other duties, 2:69-75
    outcome of consultation,
      2:69
    redevelopment scheme,
      declaration of, 2:72-73
  tenants' organisations,
    funding for, 2:78-79
  See also Information
Contingency fees

Entries in this volume appear in bold.
1. *Security of Tenure* 2. *Tenants' Rights* 3. *Nuisance and Harassment*
4. *Presenting Possession Proceedings* 5. *Repairs and Maintenance*
6. *Dealing with Disrepair*

environmental protection,
relating to, 5:103-104
Contract
breach of, limitation periods,
5:78
repairing obligation of social
landlord. *See* Repairs and
maintenance
Contractual succession clauses
alternative approach, 2:29-30
enforceability of right of
assignment, 2:28-29
generally, 2:26
housing association, 2:26-27
local authority, 2:27-28, 2:29
Costs
environmental protection,
relating to, 5:102-103
possession proceedings. *See*
Possession proceedings
repair, litigation relating to,
5:2-3, 5:102-103
Counterclaims
disrepair, for, 1:100-101
set-off and, 5:82-83
County court
accelerated procedure in,
1:108, 4:114
application to set aside,
1:123-124
rules, 3:3
squatters, procedure relating
to, 1:113
suspended order, powers
relating to, 1:120-121
trespassers, procedure
relating to, 1:113
Court
choice of, possession
proceedings, 4:13-14
commencing possession
proceedings, 4:13-14
county. *See* County court
disrepair, dealing with. *See*
Disrepair
repairs, proceedings relating

to. *See* Repairs and
maintenance
Covenants
meaning, 3:99-100, 4:155
quiet enjoyment, for, breach
of, 5:38, 5:46-47
right to buy, harassment and,
3:87
Cross-examination
meaning, 4:155
possession proceedings,
4:79-80
Crown Prosecution Service
(CPS)
criminal proceedings, 3:78
Crown tenancy
assured tenancy, exclusion
from, 1:41

Damage
private nuisance and, 3:18
Damages
general, 5:73-76
interest, 5:77
landlord's remedy for breach,
5:111-112
redecoration, for, 5:76-77
repairing obligations, failure
to comply with, 5:71-77
special, 5:72-73
Damp
complaints relating to, 5:53-57
condensation, 5:56-57
lateral penetration, 6:39-40
moisture generation by users,
6:54
moisture meter, 6:75-76
penetrating, 5:53-55
rising, 5:55-56, 6:38-39
salts and residual dampness,
6:42-43
Damp-proofing
basements, 6:19
bridging, 6:41
generally, 6:18
ground floors, 6:19

Entries in this volume appear in bold.
1. *Security of Tenure* 2. *Tenants' Rights* 3. *Nuisance and Harassment*
4. *Presenting Possession Proceedings* 5. *Repairs and Maintenance*
6. *Dealing with Disrepair*

remedial, 6:40-41
walls, 6:18
Dampness. *See* Damp
Dangerous premises
private nuisance, as, 3:17
Dealing with disrepair. *See* Disrepair
Deceased tenant
successor, as, 2:19-21
Deception
tenancy obtained by, 1:75-76
Decorations
redecoration,
damages for, 5:76-77
repairing obligation and, 5:31
Defective premises
notice, 5:41-43
premises, meaning, 5:43-44
relevant defect, meaning, 5:40-41
social landlord's non-contractual liabilities, 5:38, 5:39-44, 5:47-48
Defects. *See* Disrepair
Defences
possession proceedings. *See* Possession proceedings
private nuisance, action for, generally, 3:21
ignorance, 3:22
inevitable accident, 3:21-22
statutory authorisation, 3:22
Deliberate action
private nuisance, as, 3:17
Deterioration
furniture, of, 1:73-75, 1:88
possession proceedings, 4:39-40
premises, of, 1:73-75, 1:88
Development
home being redeveloped, letter relating to, 1:133-134
land, 1:32-34, 4:35-36

meaning, 1:33
Diary of incidents
form, 1:143
Direct action
rent,
repairs, use to pay for, 5:84-85
set-off against, 5:81
set-off,
counterclaims, and, 5:82-83
rent, against, 5:81
Directions
meaning, 4:155
possession proceedings. *See* Possession proceedings
Disabled person
accommodation for, 1:80
Discharge
suspended possession order, of, 1:122
Disclosure
exempt information, 2:59
Discovery
meaning, 4:155
possession proceedings. *See* Possession proceedings
Discretionary payments
local authority, by, 5:125-126
Disease
insects carrying, 6:50-51
Disputes
management, 2:87-88
Disrepair
animals, disease carrying, 6:55
assessing priorities,
Chartered Institute of Housing Standards, 6:122
codes of practice, 6:119-120
general factors, 6:117-119
individual basis, 6:117
planned maintenance, 6:122-124
statutory obligations, 6:119
strategic basis, 6:117
tenants' guarantee, 6:120

Entries in this volume appear in bold.
1. *Security of Tenure* 2. *Tenants' Rights* 3. *Nuisance and Harassment*
4. *Presenting Possession Proceedings* 5. *Repairs and Maintenance*
6. *Dealing with Disrepair*

tenants' right to repair,
6:121
value for money, 6:127-128
wholesale redevelopment
or rehabilitation,
6:124-127
building diagrams, 6:147-162
bushes, 6:55-56
compliance with orders,
6:142-143
counterclaims for, 1:100-101
court proceedings,
choice of expert, 6:141-142
compliance with orders,
6:142-143
expert evidence and
advice, 6:139-140
generally, 6:137-138
housing manager's
evidence, 6:142
instructing expert, 6:138-139
dealing with,
conclusion, 6:144-145
court proceedings. *See*
court proceedings, *above*
follow-up action. *See*
follow-up action, *below*
housing stock. *See* Housing
stock
inspection. *See* Inspection
of disrepair
materials of construction.
See Materials of
construction
priorities. *See* priorities,
below
reporting. *See* reporting,
below
diagnosing building defects,
6:163-167
enemies of health buildings,
animals, 6:55
bushes, 6:55-56
climate, 6:56-58
fungi, 6:47-49
generally, 6:36-37

hazardous materials,
6:52-54
insects, 6:49-51
metals, 6:51-52
non-traditional buildings,
6:59-61
plants, 6:55-56
refuse, 6:55
sulphates, 6:46
temperature, 6:56-58
trees, 6:55-56
underground threats, 6:58
users, 6:54
water, 6:37-46
evidence,
expert, 6:139-140
housing manager, of, 6:142
expert,
choice of, 6:141-142
evidence and advice,
6:139-140
instructing, 6:138-139
external advice, 6:116
follow-up action,
generally, 6:129
longer-term action,
6:135-136
monitoring performance,
6:130-131
monitoring short-term
repairs, 6:136
redecoration, 6:132-133
revisits, 6:136
tenants' satisfaction
surveys, 6:131-132
variations of works,
6:133-134
visits, 6:136
fungi,
dry rot, 6:47-48
generally, 6:46
moulds, 6:49
wet rot, 6:48-49
hazardous materials,
asbestos, 6:52-53
glass fibre, 6:53

Entries in this volume appear in bold.
1. *Security of Tenure* 2. *Tenants' Rights* 3. *Nuisance and Harassment*
4. *Presenting Possession Proceedings* 5. *Repairs and Maintenance*
6. *Dealing with Disrepair*

radon gas, 6:53-54
urea-formaldehyde foam,
    6:53
housing manager,
    court proceedings,
        evidence at, 6:142
    preparing for inspection,
        6:65-67
housing stock,
    non-traditional. *See* Non-
        traditional housing stock
    traditional. *See* Traditional
        housing stock
insects,
    disease carrying, 6:51-52
    just unpleasant, 6:51
    wood-boring, 6:49-50
inspection. *See* Inspection of
    disrepair
instructing expert, 6:138-139
longer-term action,
    generally, 6:135
    monitoring short-term
        repairs, 6:136
    revisits, 6:136
    visits, 6:136
materials of construction. *See*
    Materials of construction
metals, 6:51-52
monitoring,
    management systems,
        6:130-131
    performance, 6:130-131
    short-term repairs, 6:136
non-traditional housing stock,
    failures in, 6:59-61
    generally, 6:20-21
    high rise, 6:60-61
    large panel systems, 6:21,
        6:59-60
    modern timber-frame, 6:22,
        6:61
    no-fines, 6:22
    prefabricated buildings, 6:59
    steel and reinforced
        concrete frame, 6:21

orders, compliance with,
    6:142-143
plants, 6:55-56
possession proceedings,
    4:92-93
post-inspection practice. *See*
    Inspection of disrepair
priorities,
    assessing, 6:117-128
    external advice, 6:116
    generally, 6:115-116
    specification for repairs,
        6:116-117
redecoration, 6:132-133
refuse, 6:55
reporting,
    core section, 6:106-111
    customers, 6:104
    findings, 6:104-105
    format, 6:106-114
    generally, 6:103
    landlord's liability,
        6:113-114
    record note, 6:112-113
    reference to further action,
        6:114
    schedule of defects and
        repairs, 6:107-111
    supplementary sections,
        6:112
    tenant's liability, 6:114
short-term repairs, 6:136
specification for repairs,
    6:116-117
sulphates, 6:46
temperature and climate,
    drought, 6:56-57
    frost, 6:57
    snow, 6:57
    sun, 6:58
tenants,
    guarantee of, 6:120
    right to repair, 6:121
    satisfaction surveys,
        6:131-132
traditional housing stock. *See*

Entries in this volume appear in bold.
1. *Security of Tenure* 2. *Tenants' Rights* 3. *Nuisance and Harassment*
4. *Presenting Possession Proceedings* 5. *Repairs and Maintenance*
6. *Dealing with Disrepair*

Traditional housing stock
trees, 6:55-56
underground threats, 6:58
users, problems caused by,
  generally, 6:54
  moisture generation, 6:54
variations of works, 6:133-134
water,
  above ground, 6:43
  construction, from, 6:46
  dampness from ground,
   6:38-43
  from above, 6:44-45
  from inside, 6:45-46
  generally, 6:37-38
See also Repairs and
  maintenance
Divorce
  property transfer order, 2:32
Do-It-Yourself
  inspection of disrepair,
   6:99-100
Drains
  blocked, as private nuisance,
   3:17
  **local authority, powers of,
   5:105**
Drought
  disrepair caused by, 6:56-57
Dwelling-house
  deterioration of, 1:73-75, 1:88
  let as separate dwelling,
   meaning, 1:45-46
   separate, meaning, 1:45
   shared accommodation,
    1:45-46
  meaning, 1:44

Elderly
  accommodation for, 1:19-20
Employee
  accommodation essential for
   job, 1:24-25
  non-housing property
   required for, 1:80
  rights of, 1:25-28

secure tenancy, exclusion
  from, 1:32
service occupier, 1:24
service tenant, 1:24
tied accommodation, 1:24
Employment
  accommodation related to,
   1:76-77, 4:41-42
Enemies of healthy buildings.
  See Disrepair
Enforcement
  assignment, right of, 2:28-29
  injunction, through, 5:115
  possession order, of, 4:126
  tenants' guarantee, relating
   to, 2:6-7
Entry
  repairs, for, 5:114-116
Environmental health officers
  nuisance, powers relating to,
   3:29, 3:49
  possession proceedings,
   evidence at, 4:72-73
**Environmental protection
  Act of 1990, 5:91-104
  action by tenant,
   generally, 5:94
   person aggrieved, 5:94-95
   person responsible, 5:95-99
  appeals, 5:102
  compensation orders,
   appeals, 5:102
   causation, 5:101-102
   generally, 5:100-101
   levels of compensation,
    5:101
  contingency fees, 5:103-104
  costs, 5:102-103
  local authority duty to
   residents, 5:93-94
  procedure, 5:99-100
  residents, local authority
   duty to, 5:93-94
  statutory nuisance,
   circumstances amounting
   to, 5:91-92**

Entries in this volume appear in bold.
1. *Security of Tenure* 2. *Tenants' Rights* 3. *Nuisance and Harassment*
4. *Presenting Possession Proceedings* 5. *Repairs and Maintenance*
6. *Dealing with Disrepair*

individual 'person
aggrieved', action by,
3:28-29
local authority, action by,
3:26-28
nature of nuisance, 5:93
prejudicial to health, 5:92-93
required action under Act,
3:26-29
Estate redevelopment
consultation on declaration
of scheme, 2:72-73
generally, 2:91
housing action trust,
declaration of, 2:93-94
housing association,
local authority
development,
combination with, 2:95
sale tenanted to, 2:92-93
sale with vacant possession
to, 2:93
local authority,
housing association
development,
combination with, 2:95
redevelopment by, 2:94-95
Eviction, protection from
abandoned premises,
1:110-111
generally, 1:108
notice to quit, 1:108
period of notice, 1:109
service, 1:110
Evidence
annoyance, of, 1:72
expert,
disrepair, dealing with,
6:139-140
possession proceedings,
4:72-74
repairs, proceedings
relating to, 5:133-134
harassment, of, 3:88
hearsay, meaning, 4:156
in chief, meaning, 4:155

nuisance, of,
investigation of, 3:41-43
noise nuisance, 3:42-43
private investigator, use of,
3:42
secure tenant, grounds for
possession against, 1:72
possession proceedings. *See*
Possession proceedings
repairs and maintenance,
relating to,
experts' evidence, 5:133-134
generally, 5:129-131
housing manager as
witness, 5:132-133
specific performance, claim
for, 5:69-70
Ex parte
meaning, 3:100, 4:155
Exchange
assignment by way of,
consent, grounds for
refusing, 2:36-39
generally, 2:35
landlord's written consent,
2:35-36
mutual, 2:35-39
premium, at, 1:76
Exclusive possession
tenant and licensee
distinguished, 1:16-17
Exempt landlord
secure tenancy, relating to,
1:41
Expert evidence
disrepair, dealing with,
choice of expert, 6:141-142
instructing expert,
6:138-139
role of expert, 6:139-140
possession proceedings,
4:72-74
repairs, proceedings relating
to, 5:133-134
Express terms
implied terms conflicting

Entries in this volume appear in bold.
1. *Security of Tenure* 2. *Tenants' Rights* 3. *Nuisance and Harassment*
4. *Presenting Possession Proceedings* 5. *Repairs and Maintenance*
6. *Dealing with Disrepair*

with, **5:22**
repairing obligation, relating to, 5:16-18
Exterior
meaning, 5:14
repairing obligation, 5:12-14

Fault
nuisance based on, 5:50
Feasibility study
full, 2:85-86
initial, 2:84-85
Felt
description of, 6:34-35
Financial incentives
repair,
costs of litigation, 5:2-3
reasons for, 5:2-3
Fixed term tenancy
forfeiture, 1:62-66
meaning, 2:100, 4:155
status of tenant, 1:7-8
succession, 2:22
tenancy agreement, 2:54-55
Floors
above ground level, 6:16-17
boards, 6:18
damp-proofing, 6:19
diagrams, 6:159-160
ground,
damp-proofing, 6:19
solid, 6:17
timber, 6:17
sheets, 6:18
solid ground floors, 6:17
timber ground floors, 6:17
Forfeiture
assured tenancy, of, 1:66
fixed term tenancy, 1:62-66
notice, 1:63-64
provision for, 1:63
re-entry, right of, 1:63
relief from, 1:64-65
rent arrears, action based on, 1:65
secure tenancy, of, 1:65

waiver, 1:64
Forms
possession proceedings, 4:143-153
Foundations
brick footings, 6:12
diagrams, 6:152-154
piling, 6:13
raft, 6:13
reinforced concrete, 6:13
strip, 6:12
timber plates, 6:12
Freehold
long leaseholder's right to acquire, 1:6-7
Frost
disrepair caused by, 6:57
Funding
rent levies for tenants' funds, 2:79
tenants' organisations, for, 2:78-79
Fungi
disrepair caused by, 6:47-49
dry rot, 6:47-48
moulds, 6:49
wet rot, 6:48-49
Furniture
deterioration of, 1:73-75, 1:88
suitable alternative accommodation, in, 1:94
Further action. *See* Possession proceedings
Further and better particulars
meaning, 4:155-156
possession proceedings, 4:55-57

Gaining possession
security of tenure and, 1:55
Glass
description of, 6:32-33
Glass fibre
use of, 6:53
Grounds for possession. *See* Possession

Entries in this volume appear in bold.
1. *Security of Tenure* 2. *Tenants' Rights* 3. *Nuisance and Harassment*
4. *Presenting Possession Proceedings* 5. *Repairs and Maintenance*
6. *Dealing with Disrepair*

Guarantee of tenants. *See*
   Tenants' guarantee

Handwriting expert
   possession proceedings,
      evidence at, 4:73
Harassment
   aims of guide, 3:5-9
   anti-harassment policy,
      3:83-84
   assistance to victim, 3:88-89
   collecting evidence, 3:88
   criminal offences, 3:71-74
   evidence, 3:88
   gang-busting, 3:93
   Housing Corporation, duties
      of, 3:74-75
   injunctions, 3:78-80, 3:91-92
   laws against,
      criminal offences, 3:71-74
      generally, 3:69-70
      Housing Corporation,
         duties of, 3:74-75
      local authorities, duties
         and powers of, 3:74-82
      racial harassment, nature
         and extent of, 3:70-71
   litigation, 3:89-98
   local authorities,
      appearing in proceedings
         brought by others, 3:80
      criminal proceedings, 3:78
      duties of, 3:74-75
      financial assistance,
         provision of, 3:82
      general powers of, 3:76-82
      making bye-laws, 3:81-82
      obtaining injunctions,
         3:78-80
      promoting interests of
         inhabitants, 3:78
      section 222 cases,
         difficulties of, 3:80-81
   meaning, 3:85, 3:100
   monitoring evidence, 3:88
   obtaining possession, 3:93-98

practice in case of, 3:83-98
pre-litigation strategy,
   3:89-98
procedures in case of, 3:83-98
racial, nature and extent of,
   3:70-71
tenancy agreement,
   generally, 3:84-87
   right to buy covenants, 3:87
tort of, 3:33-35
victim, assistance to, 3:88-89
Hazardous materials
   asbestos, 6:52-53
   glass fibre, 6:53
   radon gas, 6:53-54
   urea-formaldehyde foam,
      6:53
Health and safety
   inspection of disrepair,
      6:80-81
   public health. *See* Public
      health
Hearsay evidence
   meaning, 4:156
   possession proceedings,
      4:67-69
Holiday letting
   exclusion, 1:40
   out of season, 1:84
Home
   matrimonial, 1:111-113
   redevelopment, letter relating
      to, 1:133-134
   residence condition, 1:46-51
   tenant unable to take care of,
      1:74-75
   two homes, 1:49-51
   use as, 1:46-51
Homeless persons
   accommodation for, 1:34-35,
      1:42
Hostel accommodation
   assured shorthold lettings,
      1:116
   gaining possession, 1:117-118
   hostel, meaning, 1:117

Entries in this volume appear in bold.
1. *Security of Tenure* 2. *Tenants' Rights* 3. *Nuisance and Harassment*
4. *Presenting Possession Proceedings* 5. *Repairs and Maintenance*
6. *Dealing with Disrepair*

Housing Act 1985, 1:114-115
Housing Act 1988, 1:115-118
shared living
accommodation, 1:115
tenancy distinguished from
licence, 1:17-19, 1:114, 1:115
Housing
allocation. *See* Allocation of
housing
management. *See* Management
stock. *See* Housing stock
Housing action trust
consultation duties, 2:73-74
declaration of,
consultation, 2:93
legal status of tenants, 2:94
possession, grounds for,
2:94
Housing association
committees, representation
on, 2:78
contractual succession
clauses, 2:26-27
local authority development,
combination with, 2:95
sale tenanted to,
consultation, 2:92
legal status of tenants, 2:92
possession, grounds for,
2:92-93
sale with vacant possession to,
consultation, 2:93
possession, grounds for,
2:93
secure tenants, functions
relating to, 2:4
Housing benefit
possession action, defence to,
4:93-95
rent and, 1:101
Housing manager
witness, as, 5:132-133
Housing stock
building diagrams, 6:147-162
generally, 6:1-2
information on, 2:61

inspection. *See* Inspection of
disrepair
non-traditional,
building diagrams,
6:147-162
failures in, 6:59-61
generally, 6:20-21
high rise, 6:60-61
large panel systems, 6:21,
6:59-60
modern timber-frame, 6:22,
6:61
no-fines, 6:22
prefabricated buildings,
6:59
steel and reinforced
concrete frame, 6:21
traditional. *See* Traditional
housing stock

Ignorance
private nuisance action,
defence to, 3:22-23
Illegal occupier
conditions for security of
tenure, 1:52-53
letter to, 1:131-132
Illegal user
connection between offence
and premises, 1:73
secure tenant, grounds for
possession against, 1:73
Immediate order
possession, for, 1:119,
4:123-124
Implied terms
express terms conflicting
with, 5:22
Improvements
compensation for, 5:125
rent following, 5:126
repair distinguished from,
alternative tests, 5:30-31
generally, 5:25
test, 5:25-30
social landlord, by, 5:126-127

Entries in this volume appear in bold.
1. *Security of Tenure* 2. *Tenants' Rights* 3. *Nuisance and Harassment*
4. *Presenting Possession Proceedings* 5. *Repairs and Maintenance*
6. *Dealing with Disrepair*

statutory right to improve,
  5:124-125
tenant, by,
  compensation, 5:125
  discretionary payments,
    5:125-126
  generally, 5:123-124
  rent following, 5:126
  statutory right to improve,
    5:124-125
Inevitable accident
  private nuisance action,
    defence to, 3:21-22
Informal admission
  meaning, 4:156
  possession proceedings, 4:69
Information
  accommodation applications,
    about, 2:58-59
  disclosure, exemption from,
    2:59
  housing allocation, about,
    2:57-58
  inspection of disrepair,
    preparing for,
    background information,
      6:71-73
    initial information, 6:70-71
    recording information,
      6:69-71
  landlord authorities,
    meaning, 2:56-57
  provision of, 2:56
  repairing obligations, on,
    5:9-10
  secure tenants, to,
    housing allocations, on,
      2:62
    housing stock, on, 2:61
    management, on, 2:62
    obligations relating to,
      2:60-63
    rents, on, 2:61
    repairs, on, 2:61
    tenancy files, about, 2:58-59
    tenants' guarantee, under,

2:63-65
  See also Consultation
Inherited tenancy
  possession, grounds for,
    1:85-86
Injunction
  enforcement through, 5:115
  harassment case, in, 3:78-80,
    3:91-92
  interim, 5:66-67
  landlord's remedy for breach,
    5:112
  meaning, 3:100, 4:156
  nuisance case, in,
    court, factors taken into
      account by, 3:56-59
    generally, 3:52-53
    interlocutory injunction,
      3:54, 3:55-56
    mandatory injunction, 3:54
    perpetual injunction, 3:54
    prohibitory injunction, 3:54
    quia timet injunction,
      3:54-55
  repairs, tenant's remedies
    relating to, 5:65-71
  types of, 3:54-55
Inquiries and investigations
  nuisance, relating to,
    collecting evidence, 3:41-43
    complaints, 3:39-40
    generally, 3:38-39
    giving warnings, 3:39-40
    noise nuisance, 3:42-43
    private investigators, use
      of, 3:42
    substantiated complaints,
      3:39-40
Insect infestation
  complaints relating to,
    5:60-63
  disease carrying insects,
    6:50-51
  just unpleasant, 6:51
  wood-boring insects, 6:49-50
Inspection of disrepair

Entries in this volume appear in bold.
1. *Security of Tenure* 2. *Tenants' Rights* 3. *Nuisance and Harassment*
4. *Presenting Possession Proceedings* 5. *Repairs and Maintenance*
6. *Dealing with Disrepair*

appointments, 6:78-80, 6:81-82
background information,
  address, 6:71-72
  building type, 6:72
  common parts, 6:73
  identification code, 6:71-72
  location, 6:72
  occupants, 6:72-73
  preparing for inspection,
    6:71-73
  size of property, 6:72
  tenancy agreement, 6:73
  type of property, 6:72
camera, 6:76
casual call systems, 6:78-80
conduct of,
  generally, 6:82
  introductions, 6:83
  methodical procedure,
    6:84-86
  preliminaries, 6:83-84
diary systems, 6:79-80
do-it-yourself, 6:99-100
equipment,
  basics, 6:74-75
  camera, 6:76
  moisture meter, 6:75-76
health and safety, 6:80-81
information,
  background, 6:71-73
  initial, 6:70-71
  recording, 6:69-71
making appointments,
  6:81-82
methodical procedure,
  generally, 6:84-86
  identifying defects, 6:86
  senses, use of, 6:86
moisture meter, 6:75-76
need for, 6:68-71
notes, 6:87-98
occupied dwellings, 6:68
post-inspection practice,
preparing for,
  background information,
    6:71-73

equipment, 6:74-76
housing manager, role of,
  6:65-67
need for inspection, 6:68-71
occupied dwellings, 6:68
recording information,
  6:69-71
starting points, 6:68
third parties, 6:68
voids, 6:68
purpose of, 6:77-78
reporting,
  core section, 6:106-111
  customers, 6:104
  findings, 6:104-105
  format, 6:106-114
  generally, 6:103
  landlord's liability, 6:113-114
  record note, 6:112-113
  reference to further action,
    6:114
  schedule of defects and
    repairs, 6:107-111
  supplementary sections,
    6:112
  tenant's liability, 6:114
sample table of notes and
  diagnosis, 6:88-93
starting points, 6:68
third parties, 6:68
timescales, 6:98-99
voids, 6:68
whether necessary, 6:68-71
Insulation
  description of, 6:29
Interest
  damages, on, 5:77
Interlocutory
  meaning, 3:100, 4:156
Interlocutory injunction
  nuisance case, 3:54, 3:55-56
Interrogatories
  meaning, 4:156
  possession proceedings,
    4:57-58
Intestacy

Entries in this volume appear in bold.
1. *Security of Tenure* 2. *Tenants' Rights* 3. *Nuisance and Harassment*
4. *Presenting Possession Proceedings* 5. *Repairs and Maintenance*
6. *Dealing with Disrepair*

meaning, 2:100
Investigations. *See* Inquiries
 and investigations

Job mobility
 accommodation, 1:35-36
Joint tenants
 notice to quit, 1:128, 4:33-34
 status of, 1:8-9
 surrender by, 1:126
 termination by, 1:129-130
Judge
 possession proceedings, 4:76
 reasonableness, discretion
  relating to, 1:96-97
Judgments
 repairs and maintenance,
  relating to, 5:135-136

Land
 agricultural, 1:40
 development, 1:32-34,
  4:35-36
 neighbouring, access to,
  5:115-116
 ownership of,
  proof of, 4:22-23
  tenancy agreement, proof
   of, 4:22-23
 trespass to, as private
  nuisance, 3:16
Landlord
 acts of waste, remedy
  against, 5:109
 assignment, written consent
  to, 2:35-36
 change of,
  assured tenancy, 1:42
  secure tenancy, 1:42
 exempt, 1:41
 new, acquisition of, 2:74-75
 nuisance,
  liability for, 3:13-15
  responsibility to tackle,
   3:12-13
 occupier wanted to share or

 move, 2:49
 pick a landlord, 2:74-75
 possession proceedings. *See*
  Possession proceedings
 reasonableness, interests
  relating to, 1:97-98
 repairing obligation. *See*
  Repairs and maintenance
 resident, 1:41
 secure tenancy, condition
  relating to, 1:30-38
 social, repairing obligation
  of. *See* Repairs and
  maintenance
 superior, 1:9
 works of, 1:78-79, 1:84-85, 4:41
Landlord authorities
 meaning, 2:56-57
Large scale voluntary transfers
 (LSVT)
 consultation on, 2:71-72
Leading question
 meaning, 4:156
Lease
 extension of, long
  leaseholder's right to
   acquire, 1:6-7
 long, 1:31-32
Leaseholder. *See* Long
 leaseholder
Legal aid
 possession proceedings, 4:133
Legal relations
 no intention to create, 1:21-24
Letter
 annoyance, tenant causing,
  to, 1:133
 home being redeveloped,
  relating to, 1:133-134
 illegal occupier, to, 1:131-132
 nuisance, tenant causing, to,
  1:133
 rent arrears, tenant with, to,
  1:132
Liability for repair. *See* Repairs
 and maintenance

Entries in this volume appear in bold.
1. *Security of Tenure* 2. *Tenants' Rights* 3. *Nuisance and Harassment*
4. *Presenting Possession Proceedings* 5. *Repairs and Maintenance*
6. *Dealing with Disrepair*

Licence
  elderly, accommodation for,
    1:19-20
  hostel accommodation,
    1:17-19, 1:114, 1:115
  residential, 1:10-11
Licensed premises
  security of tenure and, 1:37,
    1:40
Licensee
  meaning, 1:10
  occupiers,
    landlord, position of, 2:49
    wanting to share, 2:48-49
  possession proceedings,
    generally, 4:114-115
    summary possession,
      4:115-119
  residential licence, 1:10-11
  service occupier, 1:24
  status of, 1:10-11
  tenant distinguished from,
    accommodation essential
      for job, 1:24-25
    elderly, accommodation
      for, 1:19-20
    employee, rights of, 1:25-28
    exceptions, 1:20-28
    exclusive possession,
      1:16-17
    generally, 1:14
    hostel accommodation,
      1:17-19, 1:114, 1:115
    legal relations, no intention
      to create, 1:21-24
    service occupier, 1:24
    service tenant, 1:24
    tenancy, elements of,
      1:14-16
    tied accommodation, 1:24
  trespasser distinguished
    from, 1:113
Limitation periods
  breach of contract, 5:78
  negligence, 5:78-79
  tenant's remedies, 5:78-79

Litigation
  harassment, relating to,
    gang-busting, 3:93
    generally, 3:89-91
    injunctions, 3:91-92
    obtaining possession,
      3:93-98
  nuisance, relating to,
    alternatives to, 3:38
    generally, 3:51-52
    injunctions, 3:52-59
    order for possession,
      3:59-68
  possession. See Possession
    proceedings
  repair, relating to, costs of,
    5:2-3
Local authority
  Building Act 1984, powers
    under, 5:105
  committees, representations
    on, 2:77
  compulsory competitive
    tendering, 2:89
  contractual succession
    clauses, 2:27-28, 2:29
  drains, powers relating to,
    5:105
  improvements, discretionary
    payment relating to,
    5:125-126
  reasonableness, policy
    relating to, 1:103-104
  redevelopment by,
    consultation, 2:94
    generally, 2:94
    housing association
      development, combined
      with, 2:95
    legal status of tenants,
      2:95
    possession, grounds for,
      2:95
  residents, duty to, 5:93-94
  sanitary facilities, powers
    relating to, 5:104-105

Entries in this volume appear in bold.
1. *Security of Tenure* 2. *Tenants' Rights* 3. *Nuisance and Harassment*
4. *Presenting Possession Proceedings* 5. *Repairs and Maintenance*
6. *Dealing with Disrepair*

secure tenants, functions
relating to, 2:4-5
**sewers, powers relating to,
5:105**
statutory nuisance, action
relating to, 3:26-28
suitable alternative
accommodation, certificate
relating to, 1:92, 1:93, 1:94
tenants' management
organisation, support for,
2:83-84
**vermin, powers relating to,
5:105**
Location
suitable alternative
accommodation, of, 1:95
Lodgers
assured tenant, taken in by,
2:47
conditions for security of
tenure, 1:51-53
deterioration caused by, 1:74
illegal occupation, 1:52-53
loss of security of tenure,
1:51-52
secure tenant, taken in by,
2:40-44
London Housing Survey (1993)
racial harassment, figures on,
3:7
Long leaseholder
assured tenancy, exclusion of,
1:40
extension of lease, right to
acquire, 1:6-7
freehold, right to acquire,
1:6-7
status of, 1:6-7
Loss
secure tenancy, of, 1:122-123

**Magistrates' court
statutory nuisance in, 5:135**
Maintenance. *See* Repairs and
maintenance

Management
**appointment of manager,
5:88-89**
balloting,
further ballot, 2:86-87
requirements, 2:85
CCT. *See* Compulsory
competitive tendering
disputes, 2:87-88
feasibility study,
full, 2:85-86
initial, 2:84-85
inspection. *See* Inspection of
disrepair
proposal notice,
balloting, 2:85
right to manage, 2:82-83
withdrawal, 2:88
repairs. *See* Repairs and
maintenance
right to manage,
balloting, 2:85
compulsory competitive
tendering, relationship
with, 2:89
disputes, 2:87-88
full feasibility study,
2:85-86
generally, 2:80-81
initial feasibility study,
2:84-85
local authority support,
2:83-84
notification and further
ballot, 2:86-87
proposal notice, 2:82-83
registration of organisation,
2:89
rights acquired, 2:88
tenants' management
organisations, 2:81-82
withdrawal of notice,
2:88
secure tenants, information
to, 2:62-63
tenants' organisations,

Entries in this volume appear in bold.
1. *Security of Tenure* 2. *Tenants' Rights* 3. *Nuisance and Harassment*
4. *Presenting Possession Proceedings* 5. *Repairs and Maintenance*
6. *Dealing with Disrepair*

disputes, 2:87-88
funding for, 2:78-79
local authority support,
    2:83-84
registration, 2:89
rent levies for tenants'
    funds, 2:79
right to manage, 2:81-82
**witness, housing manager as,
5:132-133**
Managing agents
consultation on use of,
    2:69-71
secure tenancy, 1:31
Mandatory injunction
nuisance case, 3:54
Materials of construction
asphalt, 6:34-35
bituminous materials, 6:34-35
brick, 6:26-28
concrete, 6:30
enemies of healthy buildings.
    See Disrepair
felt, 6:34-35
generally, 6:23-24
glass, 6:32-33
insulation, 6:29
metal, 6:33-34
mortar and pointing, 6:28
plaster, 6:31
pointing, 6:28
render, 6:28-29
rock, 6:29-30
slate, 6:31-32
stone, 6:31
tiles, 6:32
timber, 6:24-26
Matrimonial home
cohabitees, 1:111-112
remaining spouse, rights of,
    1:112-113
right to remain in, 1:112
spouses, 1:112-113
Matrimonial property order
secure tenancy, relating to,
    2:11

Mediation
meaning, 3:100
nuisance, relating to,
    generally, 3:45-46
    process, 3:46-48
Medical evidence
possession proceedings,
    4:73-74
Members of family
succession, 2:13-15
Mesne tenant
status of, 1:9-10
Metal
corrosion, 6:51-52
description of, 6:33-34
Ministers of religion
possession, grounds for, 1:84
Moisture generation
users of building, by, 6:54
Money judgment
order including, 4:126
proof of, 4:31-32
unauthorised occupier, action
    against, 4:103-105
Mortar
description of, 6:28
pointing, and, 6:28
Mortgaged property
assured tenant, grounds for
    possession against, 1:84

Negligence
limitation periods, 5:78-79
nuisance and, 3:29-31
**repairs, relating to, 5:39,
5:50-52**
Neighbourhood
nature of, private nuisance
    and, 3:18
**Neighbouring land
access to, 5:115-116**
Neighbours
complaints from, 1:72
New tenancy
assured shorthold, 1:107
Noise nuisance

Entries in this volume appear in bold.
1. *Security of Tenure* 2. *Tenants' Rights* 3. *Nuisance and Harassment*
4. *Presenting Possession Proceedings* 5. *Repairs and Maintenance*
6. *Dealing with Disrepair*

evidence of, 3:42-43
private nuisance, as, 3:16
Non-housing property
employee, required for, 1:80
Non-traditional housing stock
building diagrams, 6:147-162
failures in, 6:59-61
generally, 6:20-21
high rise, 6:60-61
inspection. *See* Inspection of
disrepair
large panel systems, 6:21,
6:59-60
modern timber-frame, 6:22, 6:61
no-fines, 6:22
prefabricated buildings, 6:59
steel and reinforced concrete
frame, 6:21
Notice
**defective premises, relating
to, 5:41-43**
forfeiture, of, 1:63-64
**repair, relating to,
agent, to, 5:33-35
reasonable time, meaning,
5:35
social landlord's
contractual liabilities,
5:31-35**
section 48, 1:68-69
seeking possession,
assured tenancy, 1:61-62,
1:138-142
commencing possession
proceedings, 4:10-13
examples, 1:59-60
generally, 1:58-59
length of, 4:13
meaning, 4:156
secure tenancy, 1:60-61,
1:134-138
Notice to quit
abandoned premises,
1:110-111
form, 1:142-143
generally, 1:108

hostel accommodation,
1:117-118
joint tenants, by, 1:128,
4:33-34
meaning, 4:157
period of notice, 1:109
service, 1:110
tenant, by,
contents, 1:128
effect, 1:129
generally, 1:128
joint tenants, 1:128
Nuisance
agencies used to deal with,
environmental health
officers, 3:49
planning departments,
3:49-50
police, 3:50
RSPCA, 3:50
social services, 3:49
aims of guide, 3:5-9
annoyance and, 3:61-63
assured tenant, grounds for
possession against, 1:88
causes of, 3:2-5
compulsory competitive
tendering of housing
management, 3:43-44
consequences of, 3:2-5
definitions, 3:10-11
evidence, 1:72, 3:41-43
fault, based on, 5:50
inquiries and investigations,
collecting evidence, 3:41-43
complaints, 3:39-40
generally, 3:38-39
giving warnings, 3:39-40
noise nuisance, 3:42-43
private investigator, use of,
3:42
substantiated complaints,
3:39-40
invalid excuses for, 3:23
laws against,
definitions, 3:10-11

Entries in this volume appear in bold.
1. *Security of Tenure* 2. *Tenants' Rights* 3. *Nuisance and Harassment*
4. *Presenting Possession Proceedings* 5. *Repairs and Maintenance*
6. *Dealing with Disrepair*

generally, 3:10
negligence and nuisance,
    3:29-31
private nuisance, 3:15-23
public nuisance, 3:23-24
rule in *Rylands v Fletcher*,
    3:31-33
social landlords'
    responsibility and
    liability, 3:12-15
statutory nuisance, 3:24-29
letter to tenant causing, 1:133
liability for, 3:13-15
litigation,
    alternatives to, 3:38
    generally, 3:51-52
    injunctions, 3:52-59
    order for possession,
        3:59-68
meaning, 3:100, 4:157
mediation,
    generally, 3:45-46
    process, 3:46-48
negligence and, 3:29-31
neighbours, complaints from,
    1:72
noise,
    evidence of, 3:42-43
    private nuisance, as, 3:16
possession proceedings,
    generally, 4:106-109
    proof of nuisance, 4:39
    return date, 4:110
    undertakings, 4:110-112
    witness statement, 4:110
private,
    assessing unreasonable
        use, 3:17-19
    defences, 3:21-23
    generally, 3:15-16
    invalid excuses for, 3:23
    types of, 3:16-17
    who can be sued, 3:20
    who can sue, 3:19-20
probationary tenancies,
    3:44-45

public, 3:23-24
reasonableness in case of,
    1:98-99, 3:64-68
remedies, 5:50
repairs, relating to,
    fault, nuisance based on,
        5:50
    remedies, 5:50
    social landlord's non-
        contractual liabilities,
        5:39, 5:49-50
responsibility to tackle,
    3:12-13
rule in *Rylands v Fletcher*,
    complaint, matters to be
        proved by, 3:31-33
    generally, 3:31
secure tenant, grounds for
    possession against, 1:70-73
social landlord,
    liability of, 3:13-15
    responsibility and liability,
        3:12-15
    responsibility to tackle
        nuisance, 3:12-13
statutory,
    circumstances amounting
        to, 5:91-92
    Environmental Protection
        Act, required action
        under, 3:26-29
    generally, 3:24-25
    magistrates' court, in, 5:135
    nature of nuisance, 5:93
    nuisance, meaning, 3:26
    prejudicial to health,
        3:25-26, **5:92-93**
those who live with tenant,
    caused by, 1:71
visitors, caused by, 1:71
who can be sued, 3:20,
    3:36-37
who can sue, 3:19-20, 3:36-37

Oath
    evidence on, 4:77

Entries in this volume appear in bold.
1. *Security of Tenure* 2. *Tenants' Rights* 3. *Nuisance and Harassment*
4. *Presenting Possession Proceedings* 5. *Repairs and Maintenance*
6. *Dealing with Disrepair*

Occupation
  illegal, 1:52-53, 1:131-132
  owner occupier. *See* Owner
    occupier
  sharing,
    landlord wanting occupier
      to share, 2:49
    occupier wanting to share,
      2:48-49
  status of occupier,
    examples, 1:12-13
    generally, 1:5
    licensee, 1:10-11
    owner occupier, 1:5-7
    tenant, 1:7-10
    trespasser, 1:11
  unauthorised occupier,
    meaning, 4:158
Occupied dwelling
  preparing for inspection of,
    6:68
Occupier
  repair, liability for, 5:38,
  5:44-45
Orders
  compensation. *See*
    Compensation
  disrepair, dealing with,
    6:142-143
  possession. *See* Possession
    orders
  repairs and maintenance,
  relating to, 5:135-136
  unless, meaning, 4:158
Outright order
  possession, for, 1:120,
    4:124-125
Overcrowding
  secure tenant, grounds for
    possession against, 1:78
Owner
  land, of,
    proof of, 4:22-23
    tenancy agreement, proof
      of, 4:22-23
  returning home, 1:84

Owner occupier
  long leaseholder,
    extension of lease, right to
      acquire, 1:6-7
    freehold, right to acquire,
      1:6-7
    status of, 1:6-7
  meaning, 1:5-6
  status of, 1:5-7

Participation
  committees, representation on,
    generally, 2:77
    housing authorities, 2:78
    local authorities, 2:77
    rent levies for tenants' funds,
      2:79
  tenants' organisations,
    funding for, 2:78-79
  See also Consultation
Particulars of claim
  meaning, 4:157
  possession proceedings. *See*
    Possession proceedings
Parties
  possession proceedings, 4:20,
    4:138-140
Payments
  compensation. *See*
  Compensation
  tenants, to, 5:120-122
Penetrating damp
  complaints relating to, 5:53-55
Period of notice
  eviction, protection from,
    1:109
Periodic tenancy
  meaning, 2:100, 4:157
  status of tenant, 1:7-8
  statutory, 2:46
  tenancy agreement, 2:54-55
Permanent moves
  getting works done, 5:119
Perpetual injunction
  nuisance case, 3:54
Personal files

Entries in this volume appear in bold.
1. *Security of Tenure* 2. *Tenants' Rights* 3. *Nuisance and Harassment*
4. *Presenting Possession Proceedings* 5. *Repairs and Maintenance*
6. *Dealing with Disrepair*

access to, 2:58-59

Pets
  secure tenant, grounds for
    possession against, 1:70

Plaintiff
  meaning, 4:157

Planning departments
  nuisance, dealing with
    problems of, 3:49-50

Plants
  disrepair caused by, 6:55-56

Plaster
  description of, 6:31

Pleadings
  meaning, 4:157
  possession proceedings,
    4:14-20, 4:55-58

Pointing
  mortar and, 6:28

Police
  nuisance, dealing with
    problems of, 3:50

Possession
  assured shorthold tenancy,
    1:107, 4:113-114
  assured tenant, grounds for
    possession against,
    annoyance, 1:88
  breach of term of tenancy,
    1:87
  deterioration of dwelling-
    house, 1:88
  discretionary grounds,
    1:86-88
  furniture, deterioration of,
    1:88
  generally, 1:83
  holiday letting out of
    season, 1:84
  inherited tenancy, 1:85-86
  landlord's works, 1:84-85
  mandatory grounds, 1:84-86
  ministers of religion, 1:84
  mortgaged property, 1:84
  nuisance, 1:88
  rent arrears, 1:86, 1:87

returning home owner,
    1:84
  specimen form of order,
    4:150-151
  student letting, 1:84
  suitable alternative
    accommodation, 1:87
  tied accommodation, 1:88
avoiding formal proceedings,
    1:57-58
exclusive, 1:16-17
gaining, 1:55
harassment case, in, 3:93-98
hostel accommodation, of,
    1:117-118
housing action trust,
    declaration of, 2:94
housing association,
    sale tenanted to, 2:92-93
  sale with vacant
    possession, 2:93
**landlord's remedy for breach,
  5:110-111**
local authority,
    redevelopment by, 2:95
notice seeking,
    assured tenancy, 1:61-62,
      1:138-142
  commencing possession
    proceedings, 4:10-13
  generally, 1:58-60
  length of, 4:13
  meaning, 4:156
  rent arrears, effect on,
    1:99-100
  secure tenancy, 1:60-61,
    1:134-138
nuisance case, order in,
    annoyance, nuisance and,
      3:61-63
  generally, 3:59-60
  grounds for possession,
    3:60-64
  procedure, 3:60
  reasonableness in granting
    possession, 3:64-68

Entries in this volume appear in bold.
1. *Security of Tenure* 2. *Tenants' Rights* 3. *Nuisance and Harassment*
4. *Presenting Possession Proceedings* 5. *Repairs and Maintenance*
6. *Dealing with Disrepair*

tenancy agreement, breach
of, 3:60-61
waste, 3:63-64
orders. *See* Possession orders
proceedings. *See* Possession
proceedings
reasonableness. *See*
Reasonableness
rent arrears,
discretionary grounds, 1:87
mandatory grounds, 1:86
proceedings. *See* Possession
proceedings
**requiring tenant to move,
5:117-118**
secure tenant, grounds for
possession against,
accommodation pending
works, 1:77-78
annoyance, 1:70-73
breach of other term, 1:70
charitable purposes, 1:79
deception, tenancy
obtained by, 1:75-76
deterioration of premises,
1:73-75
disabled, accommodation
for, 1:80
employment related
accommodation, 1:76-77
exchange at premium, 1:76
furniture, deterioration of,
1:73-75
grounds1-8, 1:67-78
grounds9-11, 1:78-79
grounds 12-16, 1:79-82
landlord's works, 1:78-79
non-housing property
required for employee,
1:80
nuisance, 1:70-73
overcrowding, 1:78
rent arrears, 1:67-69
sheltered accommodation,
1:81
special needs

accommodation, 1:80-81
under-occupation, 1:81-82
seeking,
avoiding formal
proceedings, 1:57-58
fixed term tenancy, 1:62-66
forfeiture, 1:62-66
grounds for, 1:56-57
procedure, 1:58-62
security provided, 1:56
successor,
assignee, seeking
possession against, 2:34-35
under-occupation by, 2:22
suitable alternative
accommodation. *See*
Suitable alternative
accommodation
under-occupation by
successor, for, 2:22
warrant for, 1:122, 4:134-135
Possession orders
acceptance of rent, 1:123
application to set aside,
1:123-124
assured tenancies, 4:150-151
consent order, 4:126-129
costs,
generally, 4:129-130
interlocutory matters, in,
4:130-132
return date, orders at,
4:132
types of order, 4:130-132
enforcement of, 4:126
generally, 1:119, 4:123
immediate, 1:119, 4:123-124
leave, not to be enforced
without, 4:126
legal aid, 4:133
loss of secure tenancy,
1:122-123
money judgment, 4:126
nuisance case, 3:59-68
outright, 1:120, 4:124-125
rent arrears cases,

Entries in this volume appear in bold.
1. *Security of Tenure* 2. *Tenants' Rights* 3. *Nuisance and Harassment*
4. *Presenting Possession Proceedings* 5. *Repairs and Maintenance*
6. *Dealing with Disrepair*

arrears at significant level,
4:90-91
arrears cleared, 4:89
arrears substantially
cleared and agreement
about remainder, 4:89-90
options for orders, 4:88-92
very significant arrears,
4:91-92
rented property, 4:152-153
setting aside, 4:137-138
specimen form,
assured tenancy, 4:150-151
possession suspended,
4:152-153
summary possession, 4:119
suspended, 1:101, 1:120-122,
4:125, 4:152-153
warrant for possession, 1:122
Possession proceedings
accelerated procedure, 1:108,
4:114
accommodation,
employees, required for,
4:41-42
pending works, 4:40-41
adjournment,
court's attitude to request,
4:50
defence raised, 4:50-51
generally, 4:48
inability to prove case,
4:48-49
return date, change of
circumstances before,
4:49-50
affidavit,
evidence, 4:71-72
meaning, 4:154
summary possession, 4:116
aim of book, 4:1-3
annoyance, based on,
generally, 4:106-109
proof of, 4:39
return date, 4:110
undertakings, 4:110-112

witness statement, 4:110
appeal, 4:136-137
assured shorthold tenants,
accelerated possession
procedure, 4:114
generally, 4:113-114
burden of proof, 4:65-66, 4:154
calculation of court time, 4:64
checklists,
death of tenant, 4:33
generally, 4:32
loss of security of tenure,
4:32-33
notice to quit by joint
tenant, 4:33-34
security of tenure,
exceptions to, 4:34-37
statutory grounds for
possession, claims based
on, 4:37-43
choice of court, 4:13-14
closing speeches, 4:81
commencing,
choice of court, 4:13-14
generally, 4:7
parties, 4:20
pleadings, 4:14-20
steps before action, 4:7-8
summons, 4:14-20
termination of tenancy
agreement, 4:8-13
consent order, 4:126-129
consolidation, 4:51-52,
4:51-52
costs,
generally, 4:129-130
interlocutory matters, in,
4:130-132
return date, orders at, 4:132
types of order, 4:130-132
County Court Rules, 4:3
cross-examination, 4:79-80,
4:155
death of tenant, 4:33
defence,
case, 4:80-81

Entries in this volume appear in bold.
1. *Security of Tenure* 2. *Tenants' Rights* 3. *Nuisance and Harassment*
4. *Presenting Possession Proceedings* 5. *Repairs and Maintenance*
6. *Dealing with Disrepair*

disrepair as, 4:92-93
housing benefit as,
   4:93-95
Landlord and Tenant Act
   1987, under, 4:95
rent arrears cases, 4:92-95
return date, raised at,
   4:45-46, 4:50-51
unauthorised occupier,
   action against, 4:98-103
deterioration of premises,
   4:39-40
development land, 4:35-36
directions,
   calculation of court time,
      4:64
   generally, 4:54-55
   meaning, 4:155
   typical, 4:63-64
discovery,
   exceptions, 4:60
   filing, 4:58-59
   lists, by, 4:59
   meaning, 4:155
   pretrial procedure, 4:58-60
disrepair as defence, 4:92-93
employees, accommodation
   required for, 4:41-42
environmental health officer,
   evidence of, 4:72-73
evidence,
   affidavit, 4:71-72, 4:154
   burden of proof, 4:65-66,
      4:154
   Civil Evidence Act, under,
      4:70-71
   evidence-in-chief, 4:78-79,
      4:155
   expert, 4:72-74
   generally, 4:65
   giving, 4:77
   hearsay, 4:67-69, 4:156
   informal admission, 4:69,
      4:156
   medical, 4:73-74
   oath, on, 4:77

public documents, 4:69-70
   rent arrears cases, 4:87-88
   types of, 4:66-74
   unauthorised occupier,
      action against, 4:97-98
expert evidence,
   environmental health
      officers, 4:72-73
   generally, 4:72
   handwriting experts, 4:73
   medical evidence, 4:73-74
   surveyors, 4:73
forms, 4:143-153
further action,
   appeal, 4:136-137
   generally, 4:134
   setting aside order,
      4:137-138
   stay of execution, 4:137
   subsequent conduct by
      parties, 4:138-140
   warrant for possession,
      4:134-135
further and better particulars,
   meaning, 4:155-156
   pretrial procedure, 4:55-57
handwriting expert, evidence
   of, 4:73
hearsay evidence, 4:67-69,
   4:156
housing benefit as defence,
   4:93-95
informal admission, 4:69,
   4:156
interrogatories,
   meaning, 4:156
   pretrial procedure, 4:57-58
judges, 4:76
Landlord and Tenant Act
   1987, defence under, 4:95
landlord's case,
   cross-examination, 4:79-80
   evidence-in-chief, 4:78-79
   re-examination, 4:80
legal aid, 4:133
licensees,

Entries in this volume appear in bold.
1. *Security of Tenure* 2. *Tenants' Rights* 3. *Nuisance and Harassment*
4. *Presenting Possession Proceedings* 5. *Repairs and Maintenance*
6. *Dealing with Disrepair*

generally, 4:114-115
summary possession,
    4:115-119
limited security,
    assured shorthold,
        4:113-114
    licensees, 4:114-119
medical evidence, 4:73-74
money judgment,
    order including, 4:126
    proof of, 4:31-32
    unauthorised occupier,
        action against, 4:103-105
notice to quit,
    joint tenant, by, 4:33-34
    meaning, 4:157
nuisance, based on,
    generally, 4:106-109
    proof of, 4:39
    return date, 4:110
    undertakings, 4:110-112
    witness statement, 4:110
oath, evidence on, 4:77
opening, 4:77
orders. *See* Possession orders
ownership of land,
    proof of, 4:22-23
    tenancy agreement, proof
        of, 4:22-23
particulars of claim,
    content of, 4:17-20
    meaning, 4:157
    rent arrears cases, 4:18-20,
        4:144-147
    specimen form, 4:144-147
parties,
    commencing proceedings,
        4:20
    subsequent conduct by,
        4:138-140
pleadings,
    commencing proceedings,
        4:14-20
    meaning, 4:157
    pretrial procedure, 4:55-58
pretrial procedure,

directions, 4:54-55, 4:63-64
generally, 4:53-54
procedural steps, 4:55-62
unless orders, 4:62-63
proof,
    burden of, 4:65-66, 4:154
    checklists, 4:32-43
    inability to prove case,
        4:48-49
    money judgments, 4:31-32
    ownership of land, 4:22-23
    reason for seeking
        possession, 4:26-31
    return date, 4:47-52
    tenant's interest,
        termination of, 4:23-25
    unauthorised occupier,
        action against, 4:98
    what needs to be proved,
        4:21-43
re-examination, 4:80, 4:157
reason for seeking possession,
    landlord's circumstances,
        4:27-28
    non-secure/assured
        tenants, 4:26
    reasonableness, 4:26-28
    secure/assured tenants,
        4:26
    suitable alternative
        accommodation, 4:28-31
    tenant's circumstances, 4:27
rent arrears cases,
    arrears at significant level,
        4:90-91
    arrears cleared, 4:89
    arrears substantially
        cleared and agreement
        about remainder, 4:89-90
    defences, 4:92-95
    disrepair as defence,
        4:92-93
    evidence of arrears, 4:88
    generally, 4:85
    housing benefit as defence,
        4:93-94

Entries in this volume appear in bold.
1. *Security of Tenure* 2. *Tenants' Rights* 3. *Nuisance and Harassment*
4. *Presenting Possession Proceedings* 5. *Repairs and Maintenance*
6. *Dealing with Disrepair*

Landlord and Tenant Act
1987, defence under, 4:95
orders, options for, 4:88-92
particulars of claim,
4:18-20, 4:144-147
required evidence, 4:87-88
statutory grounds for
possession, 4:37-39,
4:85-87
very significant arrears,
4:91-92
return date,
adjournments, 4:48-51
annoyance, action based
on, 4:110
change of circumstances
before, 4:49-50
consolidation, 4:51-52
costs orders at, 4:132
defences raised at, 4:45-46,
4:50-51
generally, 4:44
inability to prove case,
4:48-49
meaning, 4:157
nature of hearing, 4:44-47
nuisance, action based on,
4:110
proving case, 4:47-52
typical outcomes at, 4:46-47
unauthorised occupier,
action against, 4:105-106
security of tenure,
exceptions to, 4:34-37
loss of, 4:32-33
service,
summary possession,
4:117-118
tenant's interest,
termination of, 4:23-25
setting aside order, 4:137-138
settlement, 4:76
short-life user property,
4:35-36
specimen forms, 4:143-153
statutory grounds for

possession, claims based on,
accommodation pending
works, 4:40-41
annoyance to neighbours,
4:39
deterioration of premises,
4:39-40
employees,
accommodation required
for, 4:41-42
landlord's works, 4:41
nuisance to neighbours,
4:39
rent arrears, 4:37-39
under-occupation, 4:42-43
stay of execution, 4:137
subleasing schemes, 4:36-37
suitable alternative
accommodation,
landlords who are not local
authorities, 4:30-31
local authority tenants,
4:29-30
proof of, 4:28-31
summary possession,
affidavit, 4:116
hearing, 4:118-119
named respondent, service
on, 4:117
order, 4:119
procedure, 4:115
unknown persons, service
on, 4:117-118
summons,
commencing proceedings,
4:14-20
content of, 4:17
meaning, 4:158
specimen form, 4:143
surveyor, evidence of, 4:73
tenant's interest, termination of,
deceased tenants, 4:25
form of notice, 4:23
physically serving notice,
4:24-25
proof of, 4:23-25

Entries in this volume appear in bold.
1. *Security of Tenure* 2. *Tenants' Rights* 3. *Nuisance and Harassment*
4. *Presenting Possession Proceedings* 5. *Repairs and Maintenance*
6. *Dealing with Disrepair*

service of notice, 4:23-25
termination of tenancy
    agreement,
    generally, 4:8-9
    length of notice, 4:13
    notice seeking possession,
        4:10-13
tied accommodation, 4:34-35
trial,
    closing speeches, 4:81
    cross-examination, 4:79-80
    defence case, 4:80-81
    evidence-in-chief, 4:78-79
    giving evidence, 4:77
    judges, 4:76
    landlord's case, 4:78-80
    oath, evidence on, 4:77
    opening, 4:77
    outline, 4:75-76
    re-examination, 4:80
    settlement, 4:76
typical directions, 4:63-64
unauthorised occupier,
    defences, 4:98-100
    generally, 4:96-97
    meaning, 4:96, 4:158
    money judgment, 4:103-105
    new tenancy, creation of,
        4:100-103
    proof in court, 4:98
    required evidence, 4:97-98
    return date, 4:105-106
    spouses, rights of, 4:98
    temporarily absent tenant,
        4:98-100
under-occupation, 4:42-43
undertaking,
    annoyance, action based
        on, 4:110-112
    meaning, 4:158
    nuisance, action based on,
        4:110-112
    specimen form, 4:148-149
unless order,
    meaning, 4:158
    pretrial procedure, 4:62-63

warrant for possession,
    4:134-135
witness statements,
    annoyance, action based
        on, 4:110
    meaning, 4:158
    nuisance, action based on,
        4:110
    pretrial procedure, 4:60-62
works,
    accommodation pending,
        4:40-41
    landlord, of, 4:41
Post-inspection practice. *See*
    Inspection of disrepair
Premises
    meaning, 5:43-44
Premium
    exchange at, 1:76
Preparing for inspection. *See*
    Inspection of disrepair
Pretrial procedure. *See*
    Possession proceedings
Principal home
    secure tenancy, 2:12-13
Private investigator
    nuisance, investigation of,
        3:42
Private nuisance
    assessing unreasonable use,
        behaviour of perpetrator,
            3:18
        damage, 3:18
        generally, 3:17-18
        neighbourhood, nature of,
            3:18
    generally, 3:15-16
    invalid excuses for, 3:23
    types of, 3:16-17
    who can be sued, 3:20
    who can sue, 3:19-20
Probationary tenancy
    nuisance, solution to problem
        of, 3:44-45
Prohibitory injunction
    nuisance case, 3:54

Entries in this volume appear in bold.
1. *Security of Tenure* 2. *Tenants' Rights* 3. *Nuisance and Harassment*
4. *Presenting Possession Proceedings* 5. *Repairs and Maintenance*
6. *Dealing with Disrepair*

Proof
    assignment, of, 2:33-34
    burden of, meaning, 4:154
    possession proceedings. *See*
        Possession proceedings
Property transfer order
    assignment pursuant to, 2:32
Protection from eviction. *See*
    Eviction, protection from
Public health
    Building Act 1984, 5:105
    drains, 5:105
    duties relating to, 5:90-105
    environmental protection. *See*
        Environmental protection
    sanitary facilities, 5:104-105
    sewers, 5:105
    vermin, 5:105
Public nuisance
    common law, at, 3:23-24
    criminal offence, as, 3:23

Quia timet injunction
    nuisance case, 3:54-55
Quiet enjoyment
    breach of covenant for, 5:38,
        5:46-47
    meaning, 3:100-101, 4:157

Racial harassment
    extent of, 3:70-71
    London Housing Survey
        (1993) figures on, 3:7
    nature of, 3:70-71
    See also Harassment
Rateable values
    high, tenancy of premises
        with, 1:39
Re-examination
    meaning, 4:157
    possession proceedings, 4:80
Reason for seeking possession.
    See Possession proceedings
Reasonableness
    breach of other term,
        1:102-103

circumstances to be
    considered, 1:97-99
council policy, 1:103-104
generally, 1:96
granting possession, 3:64-68
judge's discretion, 1:96-97
landlord, interests of, 1:97-98
nuisance cases, 1:98-99,
    3:64-68
possession, reason for
    seeking, 4:26-28
private nuisance,
    assessing unreasonable
        use, 3:17-19
    behaviour of perpetrator,
        3:18
    damage, 3:18
    neighbourhood, nature of,
        3:18
reasonable time, meaning,
    5:35
remedying breach, 1:102-103
rent arrears,
    amount, 1:99
    disrepair, counterclaims
        for, 1:100-101
    example, 1:101-102
    generally, 1:99
    housing benefit, rent and,
        1:101
    notice seeking possession,
        effect of, 1:99-100
    reasons for arrears, 1:100
    suspended orders, 1:101
repair, legal requirements
    relating to, 5:5-6
tenant, interests of, 1:97
Receiver
    appointment of, 5:88-89
Records
    inspection of disrepair,
        preparing for, 6:69-71
Redecoration
    damages for, 5:76-77
    disrepair, dealing with,
        6:132-133

Entries in this volume appear in bold.
1. *Security of Tenure* 2. *Tenants' Rights* 3. *Nuisance and Harassment*
4. *Presenting Possession Proceedings* 5. *Repairs and Maintenance*
6. *Dealing with Disrepair*

repairing obligation and, 5:31
Redevelopment. *See* Estate
   redevelopment
Refuse
   disposal of, 6:55
Registration
   tenants' management
      organisation, of, 2:89
Remedies
   breach of other term,
      1:102-103
   nuisance, for, 5:50
   repairs, relating to,
      damages, 5:71-77
      direct action, 5:81-85
      duty to mitigate, 5:79-81
      injunctions, 5:65-71
      limitation periods, 5:78-79
      manager, appointment of,
         5:88-89
      nuisance, 5:50
      receiver, appointment of,
         5:88-89
      right to repair, 5:85-88
      secure tenants, rights of,
         5:85-88
      specific performance,
         5:65-71
      tenant, of, 5:64-89
Render
   description of, 6:28-29
Rent arrears
   earlier, 1:68
   forfeiture action based on,
      1:65
   letter to tenant with, 1:132
   possession,
      discretionary grounds, 1:87
      mandatory grounds, 1:86
      proceedings. *See* Possession
         proceedings
   reasonableness relating to,
      amount, 1:99
      counterclaims for disrepair,
         1:100-101
      example, 1:101-102
      generally, 1:99

housing benefit, rent and,
   1:101
notice seeking possession,
   effect of, 1:99-100
reasons for arrears, 1:100
suspended orders, 1:101
reasons for, 1:100
section 48 notice, 1:68-69
secure tenant, grounds for
   possession against, 1:67-69
Rents
   arrears. *See* **Rent arrears**
   improvement, following,
      5:126
   repairs, use to pay for, 5:84-85
   secure tenants, information
      to, 2:61
   set-off against, 5:81
   tenants' funds, rent levies for,
      2:79
Repairs and maintenance
   access to neighbouring land,
      5:115-116
   acts of waste, 5:108-109
   agent,
      liability of, 5:10-11
      notice to, 5:33-35
   asbestos, 5:59-60
   breach , landlord's remedies
      for,
      damages, 5:111-112
      generally, 5:109-110
      injunctions, 5:112
      possession of premises,
         5:110-111
   breach of contract, 5:78
   breach of covenant for quiet
      enjoyment, 5:38, 5:46-47
   cockroaches, 5:60-63
   common parts liability,
      5:22-24
   complaints,
      asbestos, 5:59-60
      cockroaches, 5:60-63
      common types of, 5:53-63
      damp, 5:53-57
      insect infestation, 5:60-63

Entries in this volume appear in bold.
1. *Security of Tenure* 2. *Tenants' Rights* 3. *Nuisance and Harassment*
4. *Presenting Possession Proceedings* 5. *Repairs and Maintenance*
6. *Dealing with Disrepair*

roofs, 5:58-59
subsidence, 5:57-58
condensation dampness,
    5:56-57
contractual liabilities of social
landlord,
    agent, liability of, 5:10-11
    common parts liability,
        5:22-24
    existence of contract, 5:9
    express contractual
        obligations, 5:16-18
    exterior, 5:12-14
    generally, 5:7-9
    implied contractual
        obligations, 5:19-22
    information, 5:9-10
    Landlord and Tenant Act
        1985 s11, 5:11-16
    nature of repair, 5:24-31
    notice, 5:31-35
    repair, meaning, 5:24-31
    standard of repair, 5:14-16
    structure and exterior,
        5:12-14
    summary, 5:35-36
    who is liable, 5:10-11
contractual obligations of
tenant,
    generally, 5:106-107
    tenant-like user, 5:107
    waste, acts of, 5:108-109
costs of litigation, 5:2-3,
    5:102-103
counterclaims, set-off and,
    5:82-83
court proceedings,
    choice of court, 5:128-129
    court etiquette, 5:131
    evidence, 5:129-131,
        5:132-134
    experts' evidence,
        5:133-133
    generally, 5:128
    housing manager as
        witness, 5:132-133
    judgments, 5:135-136

orders, 5:135-136
procedure, 5:131-132
statutory nuisance in
    magistrates' court, 5:135
witness, housing manager
    as, 5:132-133
damages,
    general, 5:73-76
    interest, 5:77
    landlord's remedy for
        breach, 5:111-112
    redecoration, for, 5:76-77
    special, 5:72-73
    tenant's remedy, as, 5:71-77
damp,
    complaints relating to,
        5:53-57
    condensation, 5:56-57
    penetrating, 5:53-55
    rising, 5:55-56
defective premises,
    Act of 1972, 5:39-44, 5:47-48
    notice, 5:41-43
    premises, meaning, 5:43-44
    relevant defect, meaning,
        5:40-41
    summary of provisions,
        5:38
direct action,
    set-off against rent, 5:81
    set-off and counterclaims,
        5:82-83
    using rent to pay for
        repairs, 5:84-85
disrepair. *See* Disrepair
duty to mitigate, 5:79-81
enforcement through
    injunction, 5:115
entry to repair,
    access to neighbouring
        land, 5:115-116
    enforcement through
        injunction, 5:115
    rights relating to, 5:114-116
environmental protection. *See*
    Environmental protection
evidence,

Entries in this volume appear in bold.
1. *Security of Tenure* 2. *Tenants' Rights* 3. *Nuisance and Harassment*
4. *Presenting Possession Proceedings* 5. *Repairs and Maintenance*
6. *Dealing with Disrepair*

court proceedings, in,
    5;129-131
    experts, of, 5:133-134
    housing manager, of,
    5:132-133
existence of contract, 5:9
experts' evidence, 5:133-134
express contractual
    obligations,
    implied obligations,
        conflict with, 5:22
    interpretation of express
        terms, 5:16-18
    social landlord, of, 5:16-18
exterior, 5:12-14
failure to carry out works,
    5:70-71
financial incentives,
    costs of litigation, 5:2-3
    generally, 5:2
getting works done, 5:113-122
housing manager as witness,
    5:132-133
implied contractual
    obligations,
    express terms, conflict
        with, 5:22
    repair v. renewal, 5:19-22
    social landlord, of, 5:19-22
improvement distinguished
    from repair,
        alternative tests, 5:30-31
        generally, 5:25
        test, 5:25-30
improvements,
    generally, 5:123
    social landlord, by,
    5:126-127
    tenant, by, 5:123-126
information on, 5:9-10
injunctions,
    enforcement through, 5:115
    failure to carry out works,
        5:70-71
    generally, 5:65-66
    interim, 5:66-67
    landlord's remedy for

breach, 5:112
insect infestation, 5:60-63
inspecting disrepair. *See*
    Disrepair
judgments, 5:135-136
Landlord and Tenant Act 1985,
    applicability of s11,
        5:11-12
    applicability of s8, 5:45-46
    exclusions, 5:12
    pre-October 24, 1961, 5:12
    standard of repair, 5:14-16
    structure and exterior,
        5:12-14
legal requirements,
    generally, 5:4
    reasonableness, 5:5-6
    social landlords, 5:4-5
limitation periods,
    breach of contract, 5:78
    negligence, 5:78-79
    tenant's remedy, as, 5:78-79
litigation, costs of, 5:2-3,
    5:102-103
magistrates' court, statutory
    nuisance in, 5:135
manager, appointment of,
    5:88-89
materials of construction. *See*
    Materials of construction
nature of repair,
    alternative tests, 5:30-31
    generally, 5:24-25
    improvement
        distinguished from
        repair, 5:25
    redecoration, 5:31
    test, 5:25-30
negligence,
    limitation periods,
        5:78-79
    social landlord's non-
        contractual liabilities,
        5:39, 5:50-52
neighbouring land, access to,
    5:115-116
non-contractual liabilities of

Entries in this volume appear in bold.
1. *Security of Tenure* 2. *Tenants' Rights* 3. *Nuisance and Harassment*
4. *Presenting Possession Proceedings* 5. *Repairs and Maintenance*
6. *Dealing with Disrepair*

social landlord,
Defective Premises Act
1972, 5:39-44, 5:47-48
generally, 5:37-39
Landlord and Tenant Act
1985 s8, 5:45-46
negligence, 5:39, 5:50-52
nuisance, 5:39, 5:49-50
Occupiers' Liability Act
1957, 5:44-45
quiet enjoyment, breach of
covenant for, 5:46-47
notice,
agent, to, 5:33-35
defective premises, relating
to, 5:41-43
disrepair, of, 5:31-35
reasonable time, 5:35
nuisance,
fault, based on, 5:50
magistrates' court,
statutory nuisance in,
5:135
non-contractual liabilities,
5:39, 5:49-50
remedies, 5:50
occupier, liability of, 5:38,
5:44-45
orders, 5:135-136
payments to tenants,
5:120-122
penetrating damp, 5:53-55
permanent moves, 5:119
planned maintenance,
6:122-124
possession of premises,
grounds for, 5:110-111,
5:117-118
landlord's remedy for
breach, 5:110-111
requiring tenant to move,
5:117-118
prescribed periods, meaning,
5:87-88
public health. *See* Public
health
qualifying repairs, meaning,

5:86
quiet enjoyment, breach of
covenant for, 5:38, 5:46-47
reasons for repair,
financial incentives, 5:2-3
generally, 5:1
legal requirements, 5:4-6
physical condition of
property, importance of,
5:1
receiver, appointment of,
5:88-89
redecoration,
damages for, 5:76-77
disrepair, dealing with,
6:132-133
obligation to repair and,
5:31
remedies,
breach, for, 5:109-112
damages, 5:71-77, 5:111-112
direct action, 5:81-85
duty to mitigate, 5:79-81
injunctions, 5:65-71, 5:112
landlord, of, 5:109-112
limitation periods, 5:78-79
manager, appointment of,
5:88-89
nuisance, for, 5:50
possession of premises,
5:110-111
receiver, appointment of,
5:88-89
right to repair, 5:85-88
secure tenants, rights of,
5:85-88
specific performance,
5:65-71
tenant, of, 5:64-89
waste, acts of, 5:109
renewal v. repair, 5:19-22
rent,
set-off against, 5:81
use to pay for repairs,
5:84-85
reporting repairs, 5:86-87
requiring tenant to move,

Entries in this volume appear in bold.
1. *Security of Tenure* 2. *Tenants' Rights* 3. *Nuisance and Harassment*
4. *Presenting Possession Proceedings* 5. *Repairs and Maintenance*
6. *Dealing with Disrepair*

generally, 5:116-117
permanent moves, 5:119
possession, grounds for,
    5:117-118
security of tenure, 5:118
temporary moves,
    5:119-120
right to repair,
    prescribed periods,
        meaning, 5:87-88
    qualifying repairs,
        meaning, 5:86
    reporting repairs, 5:86-87
    secure tenants, 5:85-88
rising damp, 5:55-56
roofs, 5:58-59
secure tenants,
    information to, 2:61
    right to repair, 5:85-88
security of tenure, 5:118
set-off,
    counterclaims, and, 5:82-83
    rent, against, 5:81
short-term, 6:136
specific performance,
    agreeing works, 5:69-70
    evidence, 5:69-70
    generally, 5:65-66
    limits to, 5:67-68
    resisting application,
        5:68-69
specification for repairs,
    6:116-117
standard of repair, 5:14-16
stock of housing. *See*
    Housing stock
structure and exterior, 5:12-14
subsidence, 5:58-59
temporary moves, 5:119-120
tenant's remedies,
    damages, 5:71-77
    direct action, 5:81-85
    generally, 5:64-65
    injunctions, 5:65-71
    limitation periods, 5:78-79
    manager, appointment of,
        5:88-89

receiver, appointment of,
    5:88-89
right to repair, 5:85-88
secure tenants, rights of,
    5:85-88
specific performance,
    5:65-71
tenant-like user, 5:107
value for money, 6:127-128
waste, acts of, 5:108-109
wholesale redevelopment or
    rehabilitation, 6:124-127
witness, housing manager as,
    5:132-133
works,
    agreeing, 5:69-70
    entry to repair, 5:114-116
    failure to carry out, 5:70-71
    getting works done,
        5:113-122
    variations of, 6:133-134
    See also Disrepair
Reporting
    disrepair, dealing with,
        core section, 6:106-111
        customers, 6:104
        findings, 6:104-105
        format, 6:106-114
        generally, 6:103
        landlord's liability, 6:113-114
        record note, 6:112-113
        reference to further action,
            6:114
        schedule of defects and
            repairs, 6:107-111
        supplementary sections,
            6:112
        tenant's liability, 6:114
    repairs, 5:86-87
Residence condition
    security of tenure, 1:43,
        1:46-51
    succession, 2:15-19
Resident landlord
    assured tenancy, exemption
        from, 1:41
Residential licence

Entries in this volume appear in bold.
1. *Security of Tenure* 2. *Tenants' Rights* 3. *Nuisance and Harassment*
4. *Presenting Possession Proceedings* 5. *Repairs and Maintenance*
6. *Dealing with Disrepair*

meaning, 1:10-11
Residents
  local authority duty to,
  5:93-94
Return date
  meaning, 4:157
  possession proceedings. *See*
    Possession proceedings
Returning home owner
  possession, mandatory
    grounds for, 1:84
Right to buy covenants
  harassment, prevention of,
    3:87
Right to manage. *See*
  Management
Rights of tenants
  ancillary, summary of, 2:3-4
  assignment. *See* Assignment
  assured tenant,
    generally, 2:5-6
    tenants' guarantees, 2:6-7
  consultation. *See*
    Consultation
  historical background,
    ancillary rights, summary
      of, 2:3-4
    assured tenant, 2:5-7
    generally, 2:1
    secure tenant, subsequent
      changes for, 2:4-5
    Tenants' Charter 1980, 2:2-4
  information. *See* Information
  management. *See*
    Management
  participation. *See*
    Participation
  succession. *See* Succession
Rising damp
  complaints relating to,
  5:55-56
Rock
  description of, 6:29-30
Roofs
  chimneys, 6:14-15
  complaints relating to,
  5:58-59

diagrams, 6:155-158
fire walls, 6:14-15
gables, 6:14
hips, 6:14
parapets, 6:14-15
pitched,
  chimneys, 6:14-15
  fire walls, 6:14-15
  front to rear, 6:14
  gables, 6:14
  hips, 6:14
  nature of, 6:13
  parapets, 6:14-15
  slates, 6:15-16
  tiles, 6:15-16
  valley roofs, 6:13-14
  valleys, 6:14
slates, 6:15-16
tiles, 6:15-16
valley, 6:13-14
valleys, 6:14
Rot
  dry, 6:47-48
  wet, 6:48-49
Royal Society for Prevention of
  Cruelty to Animals (RSPCA)
  nuisance, dealing with
    problems of, 3:50
Rylands v Fletcher, rule in
  nuisance and, 3:31-33

Sanitary facilities
  local authority, powers of,
  5:104-105
Section 48 notice
  secure tenant, grounds for
    possession against, 1:68-69
Secure tenancy
  assignment of,
    exchange, by way of,
      2:35-39
    generally, 2:32
    mutual exchange, 2:35-39
    potential successor, to,
      2:32-33
    proof of assignment,
      2:33-34

Entries in this volume appear in bold.
1. *Security of Tenure* 2. *Tenants' Rights* 3. *Nuisance and Harassment*
4. *Presenting Possession Proceedings* 5. *Repairs and Maintenance*
6. *Dealing with Disrepair*

property transfer order,
2:32
successor assignee, seeking
possession against,
2:34-35
change of landlord, 1:42
conditions, 1:43-44
consultation with secure tenants,
acquisition by new
landlord, 2:74-75
basic requirement, 2:65
generally, 2:65
housing action trusts,
2:73-74
large scale voluntary
transfers, 2:71-72
managing agents, use of,
2:69-71
matters requiring
consultation, 2:66-69
method of consultation,
2:65-66
other duties, 2:69-75
outcome of consultation,
2:69
redevelopment scheme,
declaration of, 2:72-73
exceptions,
accommodation pending
works, 1:37
agricultural holdings, 1:37
almshouses, 1:38
business lettings, 1:38
development land, 1:32-34
employee accommodation,
1:32
generally, 1:31
homeless persons,
accommodation for,
1:34-35
job mobility
accommodation, 1:35-36
licensed premises, 1:37
long lease, 1:31-32
student lettings, 1:37-38
subleasing scheme,
1:36-37

forfeiture of, 1:65
generally, 1:29
housing association,
functions of, 2:4
information to secure tenants,
housing allocations, on,
2:62
housing stock, on, 2:61
management, on, 2:62
obligations, 2:60-63
rents, on, 2:61
repairs, 2:61
landlord,
change of, 1:42
condition, 1:30-38
local authority, functions of,
2:4-5
lodgers, 2:40-44
loss of, 1:122-123
managing agents, 1:31
meaning, 2:100, 3:101, 4:158
notice seeking possession of,
1:60-61, 1:134-138
possession, grounds for,
accommodation pending
works, 1:77-78
annoyance, 1:70-73
breach of other term, 1:70
charitable purposes, 1:79
deception, tenancy
obtained by, 1:75-76
deterioration of premises,
1:73-75
disabled, accommodation
for, 1:80
employment related
accommodation, 1:76-77
exchange at premium, 1:76
furniture, deterioration of,
1:73-75
grounds 1-8, 1:67-68
grounds 9-11, 1:78-79
grounds 12-16, 1:79-82
landlord's works, 1:78-79
non-housing property
required for employee,
1:80

Entries in this volume appear in bold.
1. *Security of Tenure* 2. *Tenants' Rights* 3. *Nuisance and Harassment*
4. *Presenting Possession Proceedings* 5. *Repairs and Maintenance*
6. *Dealing with Disrepair*

nuisance, 1:70-73
overcrowding, 1:78
pets, 1:70
rent arrears, 1:67-69
sheltered accommodation,
    1:81
special needs
    accommodation, 1:80-81
under-occupation, 1:81-82
waiver of breach, 1:70
repair, right to,
    generally, 5:85
    prescribed periods,
        meaning, 5:87-88
    qualifying repairs,
        meaning, 5:86
    reporting repairs, 5:86-87
spouse of tenant, 2:13
subletting, 2:39-40
succession,
    common law, succession at,
        2:10
    deceased tenant already
        successor, 2:19-21
    fixed term tenancy, 2:22
    generally, 2:10
    Housing Act 1985, under,
        2:11-21, 2:97
    matrimonial property
        order, 2:11
    only or principal home,
        2:12-13
    other members of family,
        2:13-15
    residence condition,
        2:15-19
    spouse of tenant, 2:13
    succession to whom, 2:21
    termination, 2:10-11
    under-occupation by
        successor, possession for,
        2:22
    who may succeed, 2:11-12
suitable alternative
    accommodation,
    allocation policy, 1:91-92
    generally, 1:89-90

local authority certificate,
    1:92
needs of tenant, 1:90-91
tenancy agreement, 2:50-54
to whom, 2:21
under-occupation by
    successor, possession for,
        2:22
who may succeed, 2:11-12,
    2:25
Security of tenure
    conditions. *See* **Conditions for**
        security of tenure
    getting works done, 5:118
    lodgers, 2:47-48
    main purpose of book, 1:2-3
    meaning, 1:1
    possession proceedings. *See*
        Possession proceedings
    subtenants, 2:47-48
    summary of legislation, 1:1-2
Seeking possession
    avoiding formal proceedings,
        1:57-58
    fixed term tenancy, 1:62-66
    forfeiture, 1:62-66
    grounds for, 1:56-57
    procedure, 1:58-62
    security provided, 1:56
Separation
    property transfer order, 2:32
Service
    notice to quit, of, 1:110
Service occupier
    meaning, 1:24
Service tenant
    meaning, 1:24
Set-off
    counterclaims, and, 5:82-83
    rent, against, 5:81
Setting aside
    possession order, 4:137-138
Settlement
    possession proceedings, 4:76
Sewers
    local authority, powers of,
        5:105

Entries in this volume appear in bold.
1. *Security of Tenure* 2. *Tenants' Rights* 3. *Nuisance and Harassment*
4. *Presenting Possession Proceedings* 5. *Repairs and Maintenance*
6. *Dealing with Disrepair*

Shared accommodation
  security of tenure, conditions
    for, 1:45-46
Sheltered accommodation
  secure tenant, grounds for
    possession against, 1:81
Slate
  description of, 6:31-32
  roofs, 6:15-16
Smells
  private nuisance, as, 3:16
Snow
  disrepair caused by, 6:57
Social landlord
  improvements by, 5:126-127
  repairing obligation of. *See*
    Repairs and maintenance
Social services
  nuisance, dealing with
    problems of, 3:49
Special needs accommodation
  secure tenant, grounds for
    possession against, 1:80-81
Specific performance
  evidence, 5:69-70
  limits to, 5:67-68
  repairs, tenant's remedies
    relating to, 5:65-71
  resisting application, 5:68-69
Spouses
  matrimonial home, rights
    relating to, 1:112-113
  succession, requirements for,
    2:13
  suspended order, powers
    relating to, 1:121
Squatters
  nature of, 1:113
  status of, 1:11
State of affairs
  private nuisance, as, 3:17
Status of occupier
  examples, 1:12-13
  generally, 1:5
  housing action trust,
    declaration of, 2:94
  housing association, sale

tenanted to, 2:92
licensee,
  generally, 1:10
  residential licence, 1:10-11
local authority,
  redevelopment by, 2:95
owner occupier,
  long leaseholder, 1:6-7
  owner, meaning, 1:5-6
tenant,
  assignment of tenancy, 1:8
  fixed term, 1:7-8
  generally, 1:7
  joint tenants, 1:8-9
  periodic tenancy, 1:7-8
  subtenants, 1:9-10
  succession to tenancy, 1:8
  transfer of tenancy, 1:8
  written agreement, 1:8
trespasser, 1:11
Statutory authorisation
  private nuisance action,
    defence to, 3:22
Statutory grounds for
  possession. *See* Possession
    proceedings
Statutory nuisance
  circumstances amounting to,
    5:91-92
  Environmental Protection
    Act, required action under,
    individual 'person
    aggrieved', action by,
    3:28-29
  local authority, action by,
    3:26-28
  generally, 3:24-25
  magistrates' court, in, 5:135
  nature of nuisance, 5:93
  nuisance, meaning, 3:26
  prejudicial to health, 3:25-26,
    5:92-93
Statutory periodic tenancy
  assignment, 2:46
Stay of execution
  possession proceedings, 4:137
Steps before action

Entries in this volume appear in bold.
1. *Security of Tenure* 2. *Tenants' Rights* 3. *Nuisance and Harassment*
4. *Presenting Possession Proceedings* 5. *Repairs and Maintenance*
6. *Dealing with Disrepair*

possession proceedings, 4:7-8
Stock of housing. *See* Housing
  stock
Stone
  description of, 6:31
Structure
  meaning, 5:13
  repairing obligation, 5:12-14
Student lettings
  assured tenancy, exclusion
    from, 1:40
  possession, grounds for,
    1:84
  secure tenancy, exclusion
    from, 1:37-38
Subleasing scheme
  possession proceedings,
    4:36-37
  secure tenancy, 1:36-37
Subletting
  assured tenancy, 2:46
  conditions for security of
    tenure, 1:51-53
  illegal occupation, 1:52-53
  loss of security of tenure,
    1:51-52
  secure tenancy, 2:39-40
Subsidence
  **complaints relating to,
    5:57-58**
Subtenants
  deterioration caused by, 1:74
  lodgers distinguished from,
    2:41-44
  security of, 2:47-48
  status of, 1:9-10
Succession
  assured tenancy,
    common law, succession at,
      2:23-24
    contractual succession
      clauses, 2:26-30
    generally, 2:23
    Housing Act 1988,
      succession under, 2:24-25
    who is successor, 2:25
    who succeeds, 2:25

common law, at, 2:10, 2:23-24
contractual clauses,
  alternative approach,
    2:29-30
  enforceability of right of
    assignment, 2:28-29
  generally, 2:26
  housing association,
    2:26-27
  local authority, 2:27-28, 2:29
deceased tenant already
  successor, 2:19-21
effects of, 2:9-10
generally, 2:8-9
meaning, 1:8
members of family, 2:13-15
only or principal home,
  2:12-13
potential successor,
  assignment to, 2:32-33
residence condition, 2:15-19
secure tenancy,
  common law, succession at,
    2:10
  deceased tenant already
    successor, 2:19-21
  fixed term tenancy, 2:22
  generally, 2:10
  Housing Act 1985,
    succession under, 2:11-21,
    2:97
  matrimonial property
    order, 2:11
  only or principal home,
    2:12-13
  other members of family,
    2:13-15
  residence condition, 2:15-19
  spouse of tenant, 2:13
  succession to whom, 2:21
  termination, 2:10-11
  under-occupation by
    successor, possession for,
    2:22
  who may succeed, 2:11-12
spouse of tenant, 2:13
successor assignee, seeking

Entries in this volume appear in bold.
1. *Security of Tenure* 2. *Tenants' Rights* 3. *Nuisance and Harassment*
4. *Presenting Possession Proceedings* 5. *Repairs and Maintenance*
6. *Dealing with Disrepair*

possession against,
2:34-35
to whom, 2:21
under-occupation by
successor, possession for,
2:22
who may succeed, 2:11-12,
2:25
Suitable alternative
accommodation
assured tenant,
comparison with local
authority practice, 1:94
furniture, 1:94
generally, 1:93
local authority certificate,
1:93
location, 1:95
reluctant tenants, 1:94-95
suitability, 1:93-94
generally, 1:89
possession,
discretionary grounds for,
1:87
proceedings, 4:28-31
secure tenant,
allocation policy, 1:91-92
generally, 1:89-90
local authority certificate,
1:92
needs of, 1:90-91
Sulphates
disrepair caused by, 6:46
Summary possession. *See*
Possession proceedings
Summons
commencing possession
proceedings, 4:14-20
meaning, 4:158
possession proceedings,
commencing proceedings,
4:14-20
content, 4:17
specimen form, 4:143
Sun
disrepair caused by, 6:58
Surrender

agreement to surrender,
1:125
conditions for security of
tenure, 1:53-54
examples, 1:126-128
joint tenants, by, 1:126
nature of, 1:125
operation of law, by, 1:126
Surveyor
possession proceedings,
evidence at, 4:73
Suspended order
court, powers of, 1:120-121
discharge, 1:122
nature of, 1:120
possession, for, 1:101,
1:120-122, 4:125, 4:152-153
rent arrears case, 1:101
spouses, 1:121
terms, 1:121
varying terms, 1:121

Temperature and climate
drought, 6:56-57
frost, 6:57
snow, 6:57
sun, 6:58
**Temporary moves
getting works done, 5:119-120**
Tenancy
agreement,
assured tenancy, 2:54-55
breach of, as ground for
possession, 3:60-61
changing terms of, 2:50-55
covenant, meaning, 2:99
fixed term tenancy, 2:54
harassment, prevention of,
3:84-87
inspection of disrepair,
preparing for, 6:73
periodic tenancy, 2:54-55
secure tenancy, 2:50-54
termination of, 4:8-13
assignment of. *See*
Assignment
assured. *See* Assured tenancy

Entries in this volume appear in bold.
1. *Security of Tenure* 2. *Tenants' Rights* 3. *Nuisance and Harassment*
4. *Presenting Possession Proceedings* 5. *Repairs and Maintenance*
6. *Dealing with Disrepair*

change of landlord, 1:42
Crown, 1:41
deception, obtained by,
  1:75-76
elements of, 1:14-16
exceptions, 1:20-28
files, information about,
  2:58-59
fixed term. *See* Fixed term
  tenancy
inherited, 1:85-86
landlord,
  change of, 1:42
  condition, 1:30-38
legal relations, no intention
  to create, 1:21-24
periodic. *See* Periodic tenancy
probationary, 3:44-45
rights of tenants. *See* Rights
  of tenants
secure. *See* Secure tenancy
Street v Mountford, 1:15-16
succession to. *See* Succession
surrender of, 1:53-54
transfer of, 1:8
Tenant satisfaction survey
disrepair, dealing with,
  6:131-132
nuisance, causes of, 3:4
Tenants
assignment of tenancy, 1:8
environmental protection,
  action relating to,
  generally, 5:94
  person aggrieved, 5:94-95
  person responsible, 5:95-99
fixed term tenancy, 1:7-8
guarantee. *See* Tenants'
  guarantee
improvements by,
  compensation, 5:125
  discretionary payments,
    5:125-126
  generally, 5:123-124
  rent following, 5:126
  statutory right to improve,
    5:124-125

joint. *See* Joint tenants
licensee distinguished from,
  accommodation essential
    for job, 1:24-25
  elderly, accommodation
    for, 1:19-20
  employee, rights of, 1:25-28
  exceptions, 1:20-28
  exclusive possession,
    1:16-17
  generally, 1:14
  hostel accommodation,
    1:17-19, 1:114, 1:115
  legal relations, no intention
    to create, 1:21-24
  service occupier, 1:24
  service tenant, 1:24
  tenancy, elements of,
    1:14-16
  tied accommodation, 1:24
mesne, 1:9-10
payments to, 5:120-122
periodic tenancy, 1:7-8
possession proceedings. *See*
  Possession proceedings
reasonableness, interests
  relating to, 1:97
repairing obligation. *See*
  Repairs and maintenance
rights. *See* Rights of tenants
service, 1:24
status of, 1:7-10
subtenants, 1:9-10
succession to tenancy, 1:8
termination by,
  generally, 1:125
  joint tenants, 1:126.
    1:129-130
  notice to quit, 1:128-129
  surrender, 1:125-128
transfer of tenancy, 1:8
unable to take care of home,
  1:74-75
written agreement, 1:8
Tenants' guarantee
disrepair, dealing with,
  6:120

Entries in this volume appear in bold.
1. *Security of Tenure* 2. *Tenants' Rights* 3. *Nuisance and Harassment*
4. *Presenting Possession Proceedings* 5. *Repairs and Maintenance*
6. *Dealing with Disrepair*

enforcement powers, 2:6-7
information under, 2:63-65
regulated areas, 2:6
Tenants' management
organisations
disputes, 2:87-88
funding for, 2:78-79
local authority support for,
2:83-84
registration, 2:89
right to manage, 2:81-82
See also Management
Termination by tenant
joint tenants,
generally, 1:129-130
surrender by, 1:126
notice to quit,
contents, 1:128
effect, 1:129
generally, 1:128
joint tenants, 1:128
surrender,
agreement to surrender,
1:125
examples, 1:126-128
generally, 1:125
joint tenants, by, 1:126
operation of law, by,
1:126
Termination of tenancy
agreement
commencing possession
proceedings, 4:8-13
length of notice, 4:13
notice seeking possession,
4:10-13
Third parties
inspection of disrepair,
preparing for, 6:68
Tied accommodation
possession proceedings,
4:34-35
security of tenure and, 1:24,
1:88
Tiles
description of, 6:32
roofs, 6:15-16

Timber
description of, 6:24-26
ground floors, 6:17
modern timber-frame
construction, 6:22, 6:61
wood-boring insects,
6:49-50
Timescales
inspection of disrepair,
6:98-99
Tort
harassment, of, 3:33-35
meaning, 3:101
nuisance, of, 3:10
Traditional housing stock
building diagrams, 6:147-162
damp-proofing,
basements, 6:19
generally, 6:18
ground floors, 6:19
walls, 6:18
external walls,
blockwork, 6:11
cavity brickwork, 6:10
solid brickwork, 6:10
floors,
above ground level, 6:16-17
boards, 6:18
damp-proofing, 6:19
diagrams, 6:159-160
sheets, 6:18
solid ground floors, 6:17
timber ground floors, 6:17
foundations,
brick footings, 6:12
diagrams, 6:152-154
piling, 6:13
raft, 6:13
reinforced concrete, 6:13
strip, 6:12
timber plates, 6:12
generally, 6:8-9
inspection. *See* Inspection of
disrepair
internal walls, 6:11
roofs,
diagrams, 6:155-158

Entries in this volume appear in bold.
1. *Security of Tenure* 2. *Tenants' Rights* 3. *Nuisance and Harassment*
4. *Presenting Possession Proceedings* 5. *Repairs and Maintenance*
6. *Dealing with Disrepair*

flat, 6:16
   pitched, 6:13-16
stud partitions, 6:11
walls,
   blockwork, 6:11
   cavity brickwork, 6:10
   damp-proofing, 6:18
   diagrams, 6:148-151
   external, 6:10-11
   internal, 6:11
   solid brickwork, 6:10
   stud partitions, 6:11
windows,
   casements, 6:19-20
   diagrams, 6:160-161
   replacements, 6:20
   sliding sashes, 5:19
Transfer of tenancy
   security of tenure and, 1:8
Trees
   disrepair caused by, 6:55-56
Trespass to land
   private nuisance, as, 3:16
Trespasser
   county court procedure, 1:113
   licensee distinguished from, 1:113
   meaning, 1:11
   nature of, 1:113
   status of, 1:11
   unauthorised occupier, meaning, 4:158
   See also Unauthorised occupier
Trial
   possession proceedings. *See* Possession proceedings
Two homes
   security of tenure, conditions for, 1:49-51

Unauthorised occupier
   meaning, 4:158
   possession proceedings. *See* Possession proceedings
   See also Trespasser
Under-occupation

possession proceedings, 4:42-43
secure tenant, grounds for possession against, 1:81-82
Underground threats
   disrepair caused by, 6:58
Undertaking
   annoyance, possession action based on, 4:110-112
   meaning, 4:158
   nuisance, possession action based on, 4:110-112
   specimen form, 4:148-149
Unless order
   meaning, 4:158
   possession proceedings, 4:62-63

Variation
   suspended possession order, terms of, 1:121
Vermin
  cockroaches,
    complaints relating to, 5:60-63
    private nuisance, as, 3:17
  insect infestation, 5:60-63, 6:49-51
  local authority, powers of, 5:105
Victim
   harassment, of, assistance to, 3:88-89
Voids
   preparing for inspection of, 6:68

Waiver of breach
   forfeiture and, 1:64
   secure tenant, grounds for possession against, 1:70
Walls
   blockwork, 6:11
   cavity brickwork, 6:10
   cavity construction for, 6:44-45
   damp-proofing, 6:18

Entries in this volume appear in bold.
1. *Security of Tenure* 2. *Tenants' Rights* 3. *Nuisance and Harassment*
4. *Presenting Possession Proceedings* 5. *Repairs and Maintenance*
6. *Dealing with Disrepair*

diagrams, 6:148-151
external,
blockwork, 6:11
cavity brickwork, 6:10
solid brickwork, 6:10
internal, 6:11
solid brickwork, 6:10
stud partitions, 6:11
Warnings
nuisance, relating to, 3:39-40
Warrant
possession, for, 1:122,
4:134-135
Waste
acts of, tenant's contractual
obligations relating to,
5:108-109
possession, ground for, 3:63-64
Water
above ground, 6:43
construction, from, 6:46
dampness from ground,
bridging, 6:41
lateral penetration, 6:39-40
remedial damp-proofing,
6:40-41
residual, 6:42-43
rising damp, 6:38-39
salts, 6:42-43
disrepair caused by, 6:37-46
from above,
cavity construction for
walls, 6:44-45
generally, 6:44
from inside,
condensation, 6:45
interstitial condensation,
6:46
moisture generation, 6:54
Windows
casements, 6:19-20
diagrams, 6:160-161
replacements, 6:20
sliding sashes, 6:19
Wiring
faulty, as private nuisance,
3:17

Witness
housing manager as,
5:132-133
statements. *See* Witness
statements
Witness statements
meaning, 4:158
possession proceedings,
annoyance, action based
on, 4:110
nuisance, action based on,
4:110
pretrial procedure, 4:60-62
Wood. *See* Timber
Works
accommodation pending,
1:37, 1:77-78, 4:40-41
agreeing, 5:69-70
failure to carry out, 5:70-71
landlord, of, 1:78-79, 1:84-85,
4:41
variations of, 6:133-134
Written agreement
tenancy, relating to, 1:8

Entries in this volume appear in bold.
1. *Security of Tenure* 2. *Tenants' Rights* 3. *Nuisance and Harassment*
4. *Presenting Possession Proceedings* 5. *Repairs and Maintenance*
6. *Dealing with Disrepair*